RED
BRICK
THINKING

RED
BRICK
THINKING

MAKE SPACE
FIND FOCUS
MOVE FORWARD

DONNA McGEORGE

WILEY

A catalogue record for this book is available from the National Library of Australia

Registered Office
John Wiley & Sons Australia, Ltd. Level 4, 600 Bourke Street, Melbourne, VIC 3000, Australia

For details of our global editorial offices, customer services, and more information about Wiley products visit us at www.wiley.com.

Wiley also publishes its books in a variety of electronic formats and by print-on-demand. Some content that appears in standard print versions of this book may not be available in other formats.

Cover design by Wiley
Brick figures: © Sebastian/Adobe Stock; © brgfx/Adobe Stock

Set in 11.5/16.5 pt and Warnock Pro by Straive, Chennai, India.

Red Brick Thinking makes a compelling case for rejecting accumulated habits and tasks to free up your time and energy for what matters most. Subtraction is powerful — not just as a business tactic, but as a personal act of agency, allowing us to consciously design our lives to better align with what we value most. I loved it.

—Kate Christie, global bestselling author of **The Life List: Master Every Moment and Live an Audacious Life**

Red Brick Thinking is like decluttering for your mind and your business. It's the reminder we all need: you don't need to do more to grow; you need to do less, better. This book helped me see that clarity doesn't come from adding more to your plate — it comes from knowing what to let go of. Game changer.

—Olivia Carr, founder and CEO, Shhh Silk

Red Brick Thinking is the missing manual for modern work — practical, evidence-based and deeply human. It's a must for anyone serious about sustainable talent and culture. It's more than a book — it's a movement. It empowers leaders to lead with intention, not inertia, and to design cultures that thrive on less, not more.

—Melissa Gee Kee, Chief Talent, Development, and People Analytics Officer at Unilever

This book cuts through the noise and dares you to do the brave thing — let go. A minimalist manifesto with maximum impact for anyone ready to lighten up and lead with more purpose, power and presence.

—Dr. Margie Warrell, bestselling author of **The Courage Gap** *and* **You've Got This!**

There's something profoundly reassuring about a book that tells you that doing less isn't giving up. Instead, Donna McGeorge reframes removing things from our lives as a powerful way to reclaim our energy and purpose. Bravo to that, I say!

Donna's metaphor of red bricks is such a clear and helpful way to think about the things that weigh us down. The stories, the questions and the gentle nudges all combine to offer practical wisdom wrapped in her deep insight, cultivated through her years working with organisations and her observations about the state of work.

This book will speak to anyone who's been caught in the rhythm of doing too much, for too long. It invites us to ask better questions and to choose what really matters.

—Maree McPherson OAM, author of **Worthy** *and* **Cutting through the Grass Ceiling**

This book is insightful, thoughtful, and made me challenge myself and my current work process. Strategic subtraction — my new best friend. *Red Brick Thinking* educated me on how humans are hardwired to do the opposite, and showed me that going against this natural instinct can actually lead to more productivity. Genius.

—Steve Menzies, former Australian Representative Rugby League Player and finance broker

CONTENTS

ABOUT THE AUTHOR

Donna McGeorge is on a mission to challenge the way we work — not by doing more, but by doing less of what doesn't matter. With decades of experience across corporate boardrooms, global brands and fast-moving industries, she helps leaders and teams strip back complexity and focus on what truly drives results.

Her career is as diverse as her record collection (yes, classic vinyl). From managing theatre and concert tours across the UK to leading organisational development for Ford in Shanghai, Donna has seen firsthand how businesses and individuals overload themselves with unnecessary effort. Now, she travels the world, both virtually and in person, helping people reclaim their time and sharpen their impact through her keynotes, workshops and bestselling books.

She's been featured on major media platforms, from Channel 9's *Today* and Channel 7's *Sunrise* to leading local and global business publications like *The Age*, *Boss Magazine*, SmartCompany, *Forbes Magazine*, *Fast Company* and *Harvard Business Review*.

Her *It's About Time* productivity series of books, including *The 25 Minute Meeting*, *The First 2 Hours* and *The 1 Day Refund*, has reshaped how people approach work. Following the success of her bestselling book *The ChatGPT Revolution*, now in its second edition, *Red Brick Thinking* cements her reputation as a leader delivering smart, practical strategies for high performers.

She runs her business from her home in South East Queensland, where she does her best thinking over a cup of tea, looking out at her garden with her husband, Steve, and her dog, Prudence.

Donna believes that complexity is a choice. Work doesn't have to be hard: we just have to be brave enough to stop, strip back and simplify.

www.donnamcgeorge.com

ACKNOWLEDGEMENTS

I've been writing and publishing books since 2014, starting with a handful of self-published titles. In 2018, I released my first 'proper' book with Wiley, *The 25 Minute Meeting*, and quickly discovered just how steep the learning curve could be. With the support of an incredible team, I found my rhythm, and in 2019, I published *The First 2 Hours*. By 2022, I introduced *The 1 Day Refund*, offering a fresh way to rethink time and energy. Together, these three books formed the *It's About Time* series, a trilogy dedicated to helping people make work *work* and take back time for what matters most.

In 2023, I dived headfirst into the world of artificial intelligence with *The ChatGPT Revolution*, which very quickly reached bestseller status, with a second edition following in 2024.

Now here we are, and you're holding my 14th book, *Red Brick Thinking*, which is my 6th title proudly published with John Wiley & Sons.

Each book has marked a moment in my own journey of growth, curiosity and connection, and none of it would have been possible without the brilliant people who continue to walk alongside me.

Lucy Raymond, Leigh McLennon and the team at Wiley — thank you for offering me the opportunity to shift my style and approach and for taking a chance on a 'manifesto' rather than a 'tip book' (as one of my readers once described my other books). You have extended my work to a whole new audience, and I'm forever grateful.

Kelly Irving — you are a legend. This project came together through a deliberate, thoughtful process that allowed each idea the time and space to unfold fully. Beyond your sharp editorial skills, I've come to rely on your keen mind, your vast knowledge and your refreshingly direct approach to shaping great business books. I'm grateful to have you in my corner.

Anne Marie Hyde — your honesty, humour and razor-sharp command of the Queen's English continue to be a guiding light in my writing life. With every manuscript I hand over, I know I'm in trusted hands, and your insights are never anything but thoughtful, precise and true.

Col Fink — you got me 'red bricking' my work before I knew it was a thing.

Janine Garner — you saw something in this concept before I had fully formed and ran with it. Your enthusiasm and generosity in sharing it with your network gave it wings. I can't thank you enough for that.

Emma McGeorge — you are the heart behind so much of what I write. My mission to create better workplaces and, beyond that, a better world, is, at its core, for you. I love you, my beautiful girl.

And my darling Steve — this book came at an interesting time for us, written when you were in hospital and, no exaggeration, gravely ill. You couldn't make cups of tea appear like magic, but your love, support and encouragement were always present. I had to remove a lot of red bricks from our lives to make room for your health and recovery. Love you, babe.

BEFORE WE BEGIN

Every day, without thinking, we sling an invisible backpack over our shoulders. At first, it's barely noticeable, holding just the basics most of us carry: a few meetings, a handful of tasks, the kids and the usual expectations that come with modern work and life.

Over time, without much thought, we start adding more: another project here, a few extra responsibilities there, the growing pressure to be faster, better, more responsive ... more *everything*.

We don't stop to question the weight; we simply adjust the straps, lean in a little harder and keep moving. After a while, the heaviness feels normal and we forget we're even carrying it. We get used to dragging along outdated habits, bloated systems and obligations we accepted long ago, without ever asking if they still make sense. It becomes part of how we move through the world — heavier than we realise, slower than we should be and a little more worn down with each passing day.

When we finally consider it, letting go can seem like a luxury: something we might allow ourselves only after we've met every demand and fulfilled every obligation. What we don't realise is that letting go is essential.

The act of stopping, taking off the pack, unzipping it and choosing, deliberately and unapologetically, to leave behind the things that no longer serve us is how we create the space to move again. When we let go, we feel light enough to find new energy, sharp enough to regain our focus and strong enough to lead ourselves forward with greater clarity and intent.

When we choose to let go, it can feel extreme, like we're doing something against the grain. But the most powerful changes aren't always bold or dramatic. Sometimes, they're small — almost invisible to everyone else — and yet they shift everything.

One quiet example of this came in the 1960s, when Swan Vesta, one of the UK's most recognisable match brands, made a small change that had a surprisingly large impact.

For decades, its matchboxes had been designed with two striking strips — one on each side. It was simply *how things were done*. No one had ever questioned it, and why would they?

But one day, someone inside the company did. A frontline employee looked at the box, looked at the process and asked a question that challenged the default thinking.

What if one striking strip is enough?

And as a result, Swan Vesta removed one of the strips.

There was no announcement, no marketing campaign and no bold rebrand, just a quiet shift in production.

And nothing happened.

Customers kept buying matches, they struck them just as easily and there was no complaining, confusion or disruption... except to the bottom line.

With one small act of subtraction, the company saved a fortune. Fewer materials, faster assembly and lower costs all resulted from this simple subtraction, without changing the product's function in any meaningful way.

It didn't happen as a flashy innovation, and it didn't require a management off-site meeting, a planning session or a breakthrough. It just required someone to stop and ask, 'Do we actually need this?'

That question sits at the heart of this book.

> *Red Brick Thinking is about freeing yourself by subtraction and creating space by stripping away what no longer serves a purpose — or never did in the first place.*

Red Brick Thinking is the ability to pause, zoom out and challenge what you've always done, even when no one else is asking you to.

PERMISSION GRANTED

Agency is the quiet, persistent force that reminds you that you are allowed to choose differently, even when the world around you keeps pulling you back toward old habits, old systems, old expectations. It's the inner permission slip most of us forget we already have.

For so much of our lives, we are trained to wait:

- For approval

- For proof that it's safe

- For a crisis to make the decision for us.

Somewhere along the way, we internalised the idea that change — real, meaningful change — has to be granted to us by someone else.

Red Brick Thinking asks you to stop waiting, to notice the weight you're carrying and to recognise that not everything on your shoulders was put there with your full consent. It helps you understand that letting go is something you're entitled to do.

Agency is powerful — it's the simple, steady recognition that you are allowed to ask, 'Does this still belong?' and to answer for yourself without apology. This doesn't mean you'll have control over every circumstance or make perfect choices every time, but it does mean that you have the power to choose.

The ability to remove red bricks begins with reclaiming that right. No one else can give it to you, and no one else needs to. You don't need a crisis or permission; you only need to decide that carrying less is worth it.

This book is an invitation to do exactly that.

NOT ALL RED BRICKS ARE CREATED EQUAL

Some red bricks are easy to spot and easy to remove, giving you an immediate lift, while others are buried deep — woven into your identity, your habits and your systems. Pulling them free takes more time, more courage and more care. I call these small 'r' and big 'R' red bricks.

Small 'r' red bricks are easy edits and quick wins:

- Cancelling a meeting that doesn't need to happen

- Saying no to an obligation you're no longer excited about

- Making small decisions that return space to your life, piece by piece.

These aren't life-changing moves, but they add up. Small 'r' red bricks loosen the load, chip away at the chaos and remind us that we don't have to say yes to everything.

Big 'R' red bricks are heavier and stickier:

- Roles, routines and responsibilities you've outgrown

- Legacy systems that no one questions anymore

- Relationships that no longer reflect who you are or where you're heading.

They're not always as easy to spot, and they're rarely easy to let go of, but removing a big 'R' red brick doesn't just create space in your calendar. It creates space in your identity.

In organisations, big 'R' red bricks are particularly stubborn. They are protected by habit, hierarchy and the unspoken rule of 'this is how we've always done it' — but legacy is not the same as value, and familiarity doesn't equal fit.

The real work is in knowing which red bricks to remove — and having the guts to go ahead and do it.

CHOOSE YOUR PATH

In this book, you might be tempted to skip ahead to the chapters that feel 'relevant'. Go for it.

Start with those that resonate, and be curious about the ones that don't. Sometimes the red bricks you barely notice are the ones weighing you down the most.

You won't find rigid steps to follow or fancy models. You won't find any productivity hacks or efficiency tricks (see my other books for these). Instead, you will find ideas that question:

- What can be removed?
- What's getting in the way?
- What no longer works?

This book is about moving towards clarity, focus and impact, while recognising that progress doesn't come from piling on but from stripping away.

The Red Brick Revelation (Part 1) lays the foundation by introducing the core metaphor of Red Brick Thinking and challenges the default mindset of 'more is better'. It unpacks why we tend to add when we should subtract, and what becomes possible when we flip that instinct.

After this, we'll look at the most common red bricks, grouped as follows:

- **Cultural Red Bricks (Part 2):** These red bricks are born from a world that equates 'more' with progress: more speed, more success, more pressure. They keep us chasing when we're already full.

- **Structural Red Bricks (Part 3):** These red bricks live in the way we work and think, including hidden complexity, poor design and the resistance built into everyday environments. They create drag when we're trying to move forward.

- **Emotional Red Bricks (Part 4):** These are the social and emotional red bricks we stack through obligation, overcommitment and fear of letting others down. They're heavy and often inherited.

The Red Brick Revolution (Part 5) invites you to act: to build subtraction into the way you work, decide and lead by doing less *deliberately*.

This book is not linear, and you certainly don't need to read it from cover to cover, in one sitting. Each chapter stands alone, like a single red brick you're invited to examine and, if necessary, remove.

Red Brick Thinking isn't just a book or an idea.

It's a movement.

And it starts with you.

PART 1

THE RED BRICK REVELATION

Every movement begins with a moment of clarity.

This one starts with a single red brick.

As you'll soon see, *Red Brick Thinking* is not just a story about a red LEGO® brick. It's a deeper invitation to rethink progress, complexity and the subtle power of stopping.

You're not just reading a book. You're stepping into a different way of thinking — a smarter, sharper and simpler one that asks a powerful question:

'What can I let go of today that my future self will thank me for?'

Not tomorrow or when things calm down. Today.

No need for a grand plan, a spreadsheet, a whiteboard or a strategy meeting off-site.

One single decision.

One moment of clarity.

One unnecessary thing removed.

One red brick.

It's your move.

Chapter 1

Why a brick? And why is it red?

In 2022, in my corporate workshops, I would begin by using a simple, coloured, slightly lopsided LEGO bridge to demonstrate a key idea in productivity.

When I asked participants how to make it level, nearly everyone reached for an extra block.

A few pulled the whole thing apart and rebuilt it from scratch.

Some made it their business to incorporate *all* the available bricks.

But very few people thought to remove the *one, small red brick* at the bottom of the right-hand leg of the bridge. They didn't think to remove the one brick that was causing the imbalance in the first place.

When someone finally does take that brick away, there's always a collective 'aha'.

In that moment, we discover Red Brick Thinking: the shift from *addition* to *subtraction*.

This answers the 'Why a brick?' question. As for 'Why it is red?', in this exercise, the simple act of *removing* the red brick is the key — the revelation.

The seed for *Red Brick Thinking* came in 2021, as part of the research for my book *The 1 Day Refund*. An article from *Harvard Business Review* landed on my screen with a title that stopped me in my tracks: '*When subtraction adds value.*'

It described something I had long sensed but hadn't yet named: our default as humans is to solve problems by adding something. For example, we might:

- Add a tool
- Add a feature
- Add another process, person or policy.

The article drew from a powerful piece of research published in *Nature* earlier that year by Gabrielle Adams and her colleagues. In a series of clever experiments, they found that when people were asked to improve something, they overwhelmingly tried to do so by adding. Subtraction rarely crossed the participants' minds.

The research suggested that even when removing something is not only possible but clearly the better option, our brains tend to skip that option entirely.

That one detail made me sit up straighter.

Because I'd seen it too, time and again, in boardrooms, team workshops and leadership coaching sessions.

> *When faced with problems, we throw 'more' at them. What happens when we ask: 'What can I remove?'*

THE CASE FOR LETTING GO

We've been conditioned to associate progress with accumulation.

Our calendars fill up, our strategies get bloated, our products grow unwieldy and our brains get overloaded, all in the name of improvement.

But real improvement, the kind that leads to creativity and performance, comes from letting go.

The research from Adams and her team gave scientific backing to something deeply intuitive: subtraction is a powerful, underused tool. In the rush to optimise, we forget the most elegant solutions often come not from doing more, but from doing less.

Think of the sculptor, Michelangelo, who said he saw the angel in the marble and carved until he set it free. He didn't add a thing; he removed what didn't belong. (More on this incredible Red Brick Thinker in Chapter 2.)

Imagine if we approached our work, our time, our lives like a sculptor: an approach not defined by austerity or blanket minimalism but by strategic, intentional subtraction.

- What if leadership was about clearing the path for others?
- What if productivity was defined by doing fewer things — and only those that matter?
- What if clarity came not from learning something new, but from letting go of something old?

This book is an invitation to rethink how we work, lead and live: to notice the red bricks and to consider removal not as a last resort, but as a first move.

WHY WE NEED RED BRICK THINKING RIGHT NOW

In 2019, the World Health Organization (WHO) officially recognised burnout as an occupational phenomenon.

For the first time, the WHO gave language to something that millions had been silently enduring for decades: the slow, grinding depletion of energy, meaning and resilience arising from chronic, unmanaged workplace stress.

Burnout shifted from being a definition to a diagnosis, and now it has a place in the international health lexicon — not as a mental illness, but as a workplace reality with real consequences.

The WHO defined it across three distinct dimensions:

- Exhaustion — not just tired, but empty.

- Cynicism or mental distance from work — the creeping disconnection from what used to matter.

- Reduced efficacy — the feeling that no matter what you do, it's not enough.

The roots of burnout had been growing for decades.

First coined in the 1970s by psychologist Herbert Freudenberger, burnout was originally observed in doctors, nurses, teachers, social workers — those who poured their energy into helping others, often with little left for themselves. Over time, however, it became clear that burnout didn't discriminate. It could hit anyone, anywhere, from frontline staff in care homes to CEOs in corporate offices.

Then, along came COVID-19 — a global accelerant that turned quiet exhaustion into a public health crisis.

In March 2022, the WHO released a stark update: anxiety and depression had increased by 25 per cent globally during the first year of the pandemic. People weren't just burnt out; they were running on fumes.

- Healthcare workers were reporting skyrocketing emotional fatigue.

- Teachers were being pushed to breaking point.

- Parents were navigating remote learning, job uncertainty and caregiving all at once.

Those already teetering on the edge, who had quietly accepted exhaustion as normal, finally fell over.

- A survey by McKinsey found that, post-pandemic, one in four employees globally were experiencing symptoms of burnout.

- In Australia, new research from SuperFriend found that 72 per cent of workers experienced burnout symptoms in the past year, with younger generations reporting the highest levels.

The workplace, it seemed, had become not just a source of pressure but a system running on the assumption that depletion is inevitable. In response, many organisations rushed to offer resilience training, trying to fix the symptoms without questioning the system that caused them.

Burnout doesn't just come from working too hard; it comes from working too hard, for too long, on things that no longer feel meaningful, manageable or aligned. It comes from systems that reward availability over value, reactivity over rest, and martyrdom over sustainability.

It was this reality, not just the headlines, that made the WHO's declaration matter. It meant we could stop victim blaming (by suggesting burnout is a personal weakness) and start finding solutions. Once something has a name, it can no longer hide in plain sight.

Burnout is a signal, like a red flag waving from the edge of your capacity, telling you that something needs to change. It's what happens when busy becomes a mark of pride and exhaustion becomes expected. In other words, burnout is the echo of a culture that's forgotten how to rest.

> *Red Brick Thinking asks: 'How do we pull back from the edge, not just individually but systemically?'*

Through Red Brick Thinking, we can begin to redesign the environments that create the conditions for burnout.

THE SCIENCE OF SPACE: WHY DOING LESS UNLOCKS MORE

While miraculous, our brains weren't built for the level of input modern life demands. In our leisure time alone, we process an estimated 34 gigabytes of information every day, with others saying it could be as high as 74 gigabytes per day, which is the equivalent of watching 16 full-length movies. Each notification, meeting, choice, tab and tiny decision pulls from the same finite cognitive pool (our working memory), and when that pool overflows, we don't just get distracted — we get worse at everything.

Psychologists call this *cognitive overload.* It reduces our ability to focus, problem-solve, empathise and even self-regulate.

A 2006 study in *Neuroscience* by a group of University of Oregon researchers found that individuals who limit their attention to fewer stimuli perform exponentially better on working memory tasks than those who try to juggle multiple inputs. Their brains aren't faster; they're quieter.

This is why subtraction matters. Such simplicity is elegant and effective.

Think about elite athletes, top performers, the world's best chess players. They don't try to see everything at once: they reduce the field, cut out distraction and zoom in on their desired outcome.

Having an edge comes from knowing what *not* to do.

In recent years, companies like Citi, Facebook and Canva have introduced no-meeting days — not as a perk, but as a performance strategy. They saw what happened when people had room to think: better decisions, clearer strategy, more innovation, less rework and fewer errors. Subtraction works.

Finland, often ranked as having one of the best education systems in the world, builds its entire national curriculum around space to think. Students spend less time in class than almost any other developed country, and yet they outperform on global benchmarks. They know that deep learning requires breathing space, and subtraction is what makes room.

In 2023, St Joseph's College in Geelong, Australia, decided to run an experiment that went against decades of tradition and restructured the typical five-day school week. Formal classes would run on only four days: Monday, Tuesday, Thursday and Friday.

Wednesdays would be completely different: no scheduled classes, bells, uniforms or mandatory attendance. Instead, students could use the day for revision, independent study, collaborative projects or seeking extra support from teachers. The staff called it a 'flexible learning day', but what it really was, at its core, was subtraction. A deliberate pause and a break in rhythm. Space.

Students didn't check out; they leaned in.

One student, interviewed by the *Herald Sun*, said it allowed him to 'slow down, catch up and breathe', a rare combination in the high-pressure rhythm of secondary schooling. Others used it to tackle homework, prepare for exams or deepen their understanding of material that had previously flown past them in their packed timetables.

Teachers observed higher engagement on the four formal class days. Instead of coasting through a stretched week, students turned up sharper, better rested and more focused. Parents noticed the shift too, with many reporting that their teens were more balanced, more self-directed and less overwhelmed.

And here's the (not so) surprising part: in many cases, academic results improved. Once the fuss of over-scheduling and over-structuring had been removed, what remained was what mattered: real thinking, real learning and real attention.

Red Brick Thinking is having the courage to ask, 'Is this structure still serving the outcome?' — and if the answer is no, to remove it.

PROGRESS ISN'T ALWAYS FORWARD

In a world obsessed with optimising and maximising, St Joseph's College proved that sometimes you get better results not by pushing harder, but by making space.

And the lesson goes beyond the classroom.

- What if your work week had one day of intentional down time?

- What if your team had breathing room instead of burnout cycles?

- What if your own learning or creativity flourished not by doing more, but by subtracting just enough?

Subtraction is the quiet architecture of momentum. When the noise drops, the signal sharpens — and that's how you move things forward. It's a reminder that doing less is powerful, precise and profoundly human.

Chapter 2

The power of strategic subtraction

I n 2021, luxury fashion brand Bottega Veneta did the unthinkable: it deleted all its social media accounts. No more Instagram, Twitter or Facebook.

In an industry where visibility is everything, this was radical subtraction — and it was deliberate. The brand wanted to cultivate exclusivity and stand apart in an increasingly overcrowded luxury market, so it leaned into private, invitation-only events and allowed its designs, not its digital presence, to do the talking.

Bottega Veneta didn't disappear; it became more desirable.

In the first half of 2021, the brand's revenue grew by 24 per cent, surpassing €1.5 billion and marking a 32 per cent increase compared to 2019.

By reducing its digital footprint, Bottega Veneta maintained its allure and strengthened its market position, demonstrating the power of strategic subtraction in a saturated digital landscape.

Bottega Veneta showed us what subtraction can look like at scale, but you don't have to be a luxury brand to make a bold move.

EVERYONE'S DONE A CLEAN-OUT

Most subtraction is reactive. It happens when we've already hit a wall: when the calendar's too full, the inbox is a war zone and the wardrobe is bursting at the seams; when we're overwhelmed and the only way forward is to strip something, *anything*, back.

You delete emails, tidy your desk and cancel a meeting that you don't have time for (and likely didn't even need to happen). Maybe you Marie Kondo your sock drawer, and for that moment, you feel much lighter and clearer — more in control.

This kind of subtraction is useful, but it's rarely transformative. It clears the surface and helps us breathe, but it doesn't change the game.

Strategic subtraction does.

With strategic subtraction, we don't wait until we're exhausted; we do less *on purpose*. It's the proactive, intentional removal of things that seem useful, important, even successful, but are quietly slowing us down or pulling us off course.

If regular subtraction is a spring clean, strategic subtraction is architectural. It tears out walls to open up space, repurpose rooms and build something better.

It's uncomfortable, it asks harder questions and, often, it means letting go of things that once worked: projects that made sense, rituals that brought comfort or people you've relied on.

That's why so few people do it. But those who do create space for growth, focus and serious results.

WHAT MAKES SUBTRACTION *STRATEGIC?*

We cut things all the time without thinking: a skipped gym session, an email left unanswered or a meeting dropped because something 'more important' came up.

Strategic subtraction is different because it's deliberate and purposeful. Rather than thinking about what's easiest to cut, we instead ask, 'What's the most important thing to remove?'

If in doubt, here's the test: if it's easy to let go of, then it probably isn't strategic.

Strategic subtraction goes beyond decluttering and enters the realms of design:

- It's the product manager who kills a popular feature to simplify the user experience.

- It's the CEO who stops pursuing five good ideas to focus on one great one.

- It's the team leader who eliminates a long-standing process that's no longer fit for purpose, even though it still 'works'.

Strategic subtraction recognises that every commitment, system or habit carries weight — and if that weight isn't helping move things forward, it's slowing you down. This is subtraction with intent. Does this thing contribute to where we're going, or is it just taking up space?

Sometimes, strategic subtraction means you have to let go of something that still has merit, something that's 'fine' — and that's the difference that makes the difference.

THE ORIGINAL RED BRICK THINKER

Michelangelo didn't set out to be a sculptor. Born in 1475 in Caprese, a small town in Tuscany, he was drawn to art from an early age, much to his father's disapproval. Sculpture, painting, chiselling away at stone ... none of it aligned with his family's ideas of status or security. But Michelangelo didn't care because he was chasing truth, not prestige.

By his teens, he was apprenticed to Florence's finest artists and immersed in Renaissance ideals of beauty, proportion and purpose. He learned to see not just what was there, but what was hidden beneath it.

That's what made him different. Where others looked at a block of marble and saw blank stone, Michelangelo saw something trapped inside — a figure, a form, a truth, obstructed by everything that didn't belong — as illustrated by his famous quote: 'I saw the angel in the marble and carved until I set him free.'

His work resisted decoration or embellishment, and celebrated release. His sculptures weren't created, they were uncovered — and he achieved this through removal, as well as his imagination.

The sculptures *Pietà* and *David* are masterpieces not because of what was added, but because of what was taken away. Michelangelo's genius was in his vision, precision and willingness to eliminate anything that wasn't the art.

This is more than just a method; it's a mindset. It's a belief that beauty, clarity and focus are not created by adding more, but revealed by removing what hides these qualities.

The greatest sculptors, like the greatest leaders and thinkers, don't force greatness into being. They chip away at what doesn't belong, freeing what was always there.

Red Brick Thinking asks: 'What could we take away that would set our potential free?'

IF STRATEGIC SUBTRACTION IS SO POWERFUL, WHY DON'T MORE PEOPLE DO IT?

Humans are natural adders. Psychologists call it *addition bias*: our instinctive tendency to solve problems by adding elements rather than removing them. It feels safer, more productive and more impressive.

We hesitate to strategically subtract because it's uncomfortable and it goes against how we've been wired and rewarded. Addition comes far more naturally:

- **It's cognitively easier.** Adding is straightforward, whereas subtraction requires discernment. It means stopping, questioning and deciding what no longer belongs, which demands more mental effort.

- **It looks more creative.** We've been trained to associate innovation with creation: add a new feature, roll out a new program, launch a new idea. Adding feels like momentum, whereas subtracting looks like retreat.

- **It feels less risky.** In a meeting, it's safer to suggest adding something than taking something away, whereas subtraction can feel like a gamble. (What if we cut the wrong thing? What if something breaks?)

- **It's rooted in survival thinking.** Evolution has wired us to associate 'more' with safety: more food, more options, more resources. Subtraction goes against that grain and can feel like scarcity.

- **It's more visible.** In many workplaces, contribution is measured by what you build or bring; for example, a new spreadsheet, slide deck or strategy. Rarely do we get credit for the meeting we cancelled, the step we skipped or the thing we *didn't* do.

We see it in business all the time.

- A process isn't working? Add a new step.
- People aren't aligned? Add another workflow.
- The team isn't delivering? Add a new hire.
- Sales are slow? Add a new product.

Strategic subtraction requires a mindset shift.

IT'S NOT YOU — IT'S THE SYSTEM

Adding isn't a personal failure but a widespread, systemic tendency in the way we approach challenges and problems.

And then there's ego and fear:

- Fear of disappointing others

- Fear of change

- Fear that if we stop doing something, even something marginally useful, everything might fall apart.

We associate subtraction with loss, failure and retreat. We think that removing something means admitting it didn't work, letting go of a project means we wasted time and cancelling a program means we were wrong to start it.

And yet, walking away, when done with purpose, is a power move. It's a willingness to choose now over nostalgia and impact over inertia.

THE SUNK-COST TRAP

One of the most powerful forces keeping us stuck is the time, effort or money we've already spent.

We stay in roles that drain us, relationships that deplete us and routines that have outlived their usefulness. We tell ourselves, 'I've come this far' or 'I've invested too much to walk away now.'

That's the *sunk-cost fallacy* — the irrational belief that past investment should dictate future action.

We're taught to measure the cost of letting go:

- What if we cancel the project and lose momentum?

- What if we stop the program and miss out on opportunities?

- What if we remove the meeting and something gets missed?

But here's the question we rarely ask: 'What's the cost of keeping it?'

- The cost of that legacy process? The friction your team feels every day with extra steps, slow approvals and double-handling that no one questions anymore.

- The cost of that long-standing meeting? The hours lost, minds disengaged and decision fatigue from talking in circles.

- The cost of that once-brilliant initiative that's now limping along? The energy it absorbs, budget it drains and space it takes from something that could actually move the needle.

Every 'just in case' has a hidden price tag. Sometimes the cost is time or money, but most often, it's focus or attention, your most limited resource.

We like to believe we're multitaskers, that we can keep everything in the air and simply juggle faster, but the science is clear: humans are serial processors. Every additional task, commitment or cognitive load reduces our ability to perform the one in front of us.

So be honest about where your attention is going, what's still delivering value — and what needs to go because it's no longer the best use of your time, your team or your energy. Are you holding on to things that are slowing you down?

Most organisations and individuals aren't drowning in bad ideas; they're drowning in outdated ones. And the longer we carry these outdated ideas, the more we compromise the future to protect the past.

STRATEGIC SUBTRACTION AT SCALE: THE FOUR-DAY WORK WEEK

In June 2022, a quiet but revolutionary shift began with a simple question and a bold act of removal.

What if we subtracted one day of work from every week? Not restructured or compressed ... *removed.*

Once seen as a fringe idea, the four-day work week became a proving ground for strategic subtraction — carefully tested, backed by data and grounded in the belief that doing less can lead to more.

Led by 4 Day Week Global, a non-profit co-founded by New Zealander Andrew Barnes and workplace advocate Charlotte Lockhart, the movement began as a single-business experiment. In 2018, Barnes piloted a four-day week at his financial services firm, Perpetual Guardian, to test whether focus could replace hours.

When I asked Andrew about the impact of his experiment, he said, 'We anticipated having a single article in our local paper and news channel ... what we didn't expect was the global tsunami of news stories which covered the four-day week — over 40 000 across more than 120 countries. This illustrates the major cultural impact of the four-day week. It clearly shows that lack of time — for ourselves, our families and our communities — is a major issue across borders and cultures. This is borne out by our research showing that when a company implements a four-day week, the employees value that time far higher than the amount we are actually paying for it — some employees say there is no amount of additional pay which would lure them back to a five-day week. Understanding this disparity in value demonstrates why employees are motivated to make a four-day week work.'

The pilot showed incredible results:

- Productivity remained strong.

- Engagement soared.

- Stress plummeted.

- Clients didn't notice a drop in service, while employees did notice a profound change in their lives.

That one subtraction, a single day removed, sparked a global rethink.

In 2022, 4 Day Week Global partnered with researchers from Cambridge University, Boston College and University College Dublin to launch the largest coordinated four-day week pilot in the world. Over 60 companies across Australia, New Zealand, the UK, the US, Canada and Ireland participated.

They came from every corner of the economy, from fish-and-chip shops to fintech firms, and what they shared was the willingness to ask: 'What happens when we stop measuring effort by time, and start measuring it by impact?'

The rules were simple:

- 80 per cent of time
- 100 per cent of pay
- 100 per cent of output.

As Andrew told me, 'It's not doing less; it's doing things more efficiently in less time. When the benefit of process improvements comes not solely to the organisation in the form of increased profits, but to employees in more time, it unleashes creativity and innovation across the whole organisation, often in areas which are usually untouched.'

To make it work, they had to subtract the clutter, inefficiency and distractions that get in the way of meaningful work. A working day was removed and, with it, layers of waste:

- Bloated meetings were trimmed.
- Emails were checked twice a day, not hourly.
- Teams got sharper about priorities, faster when making decisions and clearer on their purpose.

A participating UK digital agency capped meetings at 30 minutes and asked one question each Monday: 'What actually matters this week?' The difference was visible in its most profitable quarter ever.

This is strategic subtraction in action.

Success came from making space for what mattered, and the results were nothing short of transformational:

- Productivity rose by over 30 per cent in some companies.
- Burnout dropped.

- Employee wellbeing improved across measures of sleep, stress and mental health.

- Retention spiked.

- For many, profit didn't fall — it increased.

This is a shift from maximum hours to maximum value, and from work as presence to work as progress... and it's spreading.

From Australia to Iceland, where public-sector workers cut their hours without sacrificing pay or productivity, the same lesson repeats: when we trust people and subtract the clutter, they simply do better.

LESS ISN'T LOSS

Don't wait for things to break down before you simplify and subtract — choose to do so early and deliberately:

- Subtract with purpose.

- Subtract with direction.

- Subtract with belief in what comes next.

Because subtraction, when it's strategic, isn't a loss — it's a lever.

Chapter 3

Anchored by attachment

I n Buddhism, the root of suffering isn't pain, or loss, or even change itself: it's attachment, the clinging to people, identities, expectations and outcomes we can't control or keep.

It's hard to argue with.

When we expect things to stay the same and they don't, we suffer. When we hold tightly to something — a relationship, a role or a version of ourselves — and it shifts or slips away, it can feel like we're losing the ground beneath us.

What hurts most is the tension we create when we cling to what *was*, instead of moving with what *is*. We hold on to the belief that this change shouldn't be happening, and our inner voice says, 'I can't let this go' or, worse, 'If I do, I won't be okay.'

This is what makes Red Brick Thinking challenging.

WE ARE WHAT WE HOLD

It's time to notice when you're gripping too tightly and recognise the things you've convinced yourself you need in order to be whole — and then, gently, ask yourself the question: 'What might become possible if I let this go?'

Attachment often arrives quietly:

- The tightly packed suitcase of an identity we've carried for too long.

- The pair of shoes that no longer fit, but we can't bring ourselves to donate.

- The spreadsheet we update every week, even though no one looks at it anymore.

We grip, we linger and we hold our breath, waiting for something, or someone, to come back — and underneath it all is a fear that if we stop holding on, we'll lose ourselves too.

THE STORIES WE CARRY

Somewhere along the way, our nervous system has learned that predictability is safe and that holding on to the familiar means we're still in control. We hold on to the idea that safety comes from certainty and control brings peace, but science tells us that what we're protecting is our identity.

Psychologists call it *self-concept clarity* — the extent to which your identity feels defined and stable. Most of us build that clarity using things that were never meant to last, such as a job title or a relationship, which creates a version of ourselves that finally seems to make sense.

However, when life does what life always does — it shifts, ends or evolves — it shakes up our circumstances, and it shakes up who we believe we are. That's why letting go feels like grief, even when the decision makes sense. We're not just losing the thing; we're losing the version of ourselves we were because of it.

Behavioural economists Daniel Kahneman, Jack Knetsch and Richard Thaler found that we tend to overvalue what we already have simply because it's ours, which is known as the *endowment effect*. We cling to that job that no longer lights us up or that role that doesn't fit anymore because giving it up feels like losing something we've 'earned'. We confuse ownership with alignment.

Add to that the neuroscience of uncertainty, where studies show that unpredictable outcomes light up the brain's threat systems, and it makes perfect sense why we'd rather keep doing the thing that is no longer right for us than risk not knowing what comes next.

All this clinging comes at a cost, because what we're really trying to do is freeze something that was never designed to be static. Everything we love, everything we are, is always in motion — and the more tightly we grip it, the more painful it becomes when it inevitably moves.

Buddhist psychology has long pointed to this tension: not as moral inadequacy, but as a universal truth. Craving (tanhā) and attachment create suffering — not because wanting something is wrong, but because impermanence is real. In other words, everything you cling to is temporary rather than permanent.

Even the ego, so desperate to preserve a stable sense of self, joins in the resistance. Freud called it a defence, Jung called it a shadow and modern thinkers just call it the trap of certainty: the part of us that would rather perform the life we recognise than risk discovering the one that actually fits.

Red Brick Thinking helps you remember that you don't need to become someone else — you just need to stop gripping so tightly to the version of yourself that no longer feels like home. The goal is to make space for what's next, and sometimes that begins with loosening your grip.

THE QUIET EROSION

We tend to think of attachment as a quiet kind of loyalty, a noble commitment to what matters, but there's a difference between love and clinging, and between care and control — and that difference can take a toll.

- **It costs you presence.** When you're attached to an outcome, you're not here in the present moment: you're in the future, scripting how things *should* play out; or in the past, replaying how it *should* have gone. Your attention is stretched thin, always leaning forward or pulling back, while never resting in the moment you're actually in.

- **It costs you peace.** The tighter you hold on, the more tension you carry, and you can't relax because you're always managing expectations, curating your image and wondering what might fall apart if you stop holding it all together.

- **It costs you clarity.** When you're attached to a specific identity or story, you start filtering reality through that lens so you don't see things as they are. Instead, you see things as you need them to be in order to keep your version of the story intact.

- **It costs you growth.** Attachment keeps you anchored to the familiar, even when it no longer serves you. It convinces you that what you have is as good as it gets, and it makes you afraid to start again, take a risk or expand your world. It keeps you loyal to a version of yourself that you may have long since outgrown.

The hardest part is that most of these costs are invisible, even though they can weigh you down. You have a sense of something you can't quite name, like a low hum of anxiety that comes from trying to control things that were never really yours to hold.

THE GRIP TEST

Attachment slips in and makes itself comfortable until, one day, you realise your life is being shaped around something you were meant to outgrow.

- **You replay the story.** You keep revisiting the moment it all went sideways. The relationship that ended, the opportunity you didn't take, the thing that didn't turn out how you hoped. You're not remembering — you're reliving.

- **You try to fix what doesn't want to be fixed.** You're the only one still pushing, still emailing, still adjusting, still hoping they'll come around, or it will make sense, or the feeling will come back.

- **You're more loyal to a plan than to your peace.** You said you'd do it, so you're doing it — even if it's clearly no longer aligned with your needs, and it's costing more than it's giving. The idea of changing course feels harder than finishing something that no longer fits.

- **You resist feedback.** You know they're probably right, but if you let the feedback land then you might have to let go of the identity you've built — and that feels scarier than staying stuck.

- **You say, 'It's not that bad.'** You keep justifying the situation and minimising the cost to stay loyal to a version of life you thought you wanted — but underneath it all, something feels off. You're shrinking to stay inside the frame.

- **You're afraid of the blank space.** The job ends, the relationship fades or the project wraps and instead of feeling the weight lift, you feel panic: not because you lost something, but because you don't know what's next.

This is your invitation to loosen the grip and let space in. You don't have to carry everything just because you once decided to.

LOOSENING THE GRIP

Letting go may not be a single, sweeping decision. It may be more of a slow loosening, or a gentle unhooking, from something that may have been right at one point but isn't anymore. What makes it hard to let go isn't the thing itself, but the meaning we gave it and the version of ourselves we shaped around it. The part of us that said:

- This is who I am.

- This is what success looks like.

- This is what love should be.

- This is the plan I made, so I need to stick to it.

Red Brick Thinking begins with awareness: noticing the loop you're stuck in, the justifications you keep repeating, the version of the story you keep editing to make it feel less painful.

Then, there's a pause: that moment when you catch yourself reaching for something (a text, an old plan, a version of life you thought you'd still be living), and you ask yourself, 'Do I really need to hold this anymore?'

It's okay to grieve what you thought would last. It changed, that's all — and your true strength shows in your willingness to stay open and to feel the unease of the empty space left behind. You don't have to know exactly what's next, and you don't need a replacement plan or a reinvention strategy. You don't need to replace every identity you've outgrown or fill every space right away.

YOU'RE ALLOWED TO RELEASE

Red Brick Thinking doesn't mean you don't care.

You can still honour the lessons, the love and the growth without dragging the things you've outgrown forward into every new chapter. You can still be grateful for your experiences, even if you're done with them.

When you remove attachment, you are returning to yourself — to the part of you that isn't defined by your titles, your plans, your relationships or the way things were *supposed* to go.

LETTING GO, BRICK BY BRICK

In every challenge, there's a moment where we instinctively reach for more: another strategy, another tool, another meeting. But real progress comes when we choose to clear away the clutter: when we have the courage to let go of what no longer fits, no matter where it shows up.

Red Brick Thinking helps you choose what's worth your energy and identify what is no longer serving you.

Each chapter in Part 2 (Cultural Red Bricks), Part 3 (Structural Red Bricks) and Part 4 (Emotional Red Bricks) explores a different red brick in our lives. These red bricks represent the habits, assumptions, systems and stories we've been taught to build with and hold on to — and Red Brick Thinking helps us identify which of these bricks are holding us back.

Don't tackle every brick at once. Some will feel familiar, others will sting a little and a few might pass by unnoticed, and for now that's okay. Start with the ones that tug at you — those that murmur, *'You don't need this anymore.'*

Notice where the heaviness is coming from. You have a choice: keep carrying what drains you, or set it down and make space for what truly matters. The most powerful thing you can do is trust that what's meant for you doesn't require you to grip so tightly.

It's time to let the red bricks go.

PART 2
CULTURAL RED BRICKS

Habits aren't built in a vacuum. We build them in a culture that shouts 'more' from every corner.

Cultural Red Bricks are the expectations we absorb without even realising. They come disguised as ambition, responsibility or even self-care, but underneath, they carry the weight of endless striving.

These red bricks are systemic.

They shape how we measure success, how we spend our time and what we believe we need in order to feel 'enough'.

They reward busyness and applaud the grind even when it's making us miserable.

In this part of the book, you'll meet five of the most common Cultural Red Bricks:

- More
- Hustle
- Someday
- Accumulation
- Perfectionism.

Each one carries an invisible cost, and we can let go of each of these red bricks when we decide to rewrite the story we've been handed.

Chapter 4

More

In the year 2000, Starbucks arrived in Australia, riding the high of global success. The company had expanded rapidly across the United States and into international markets, building a reputation not just for coffee but for creating a distinct 'third place'—a space between home and work where people could connect, linger and caffeinate.

On paper, Australia looked like an obvious next step, being a modern, affluent, English-speaking nation with a strong café culture and a love of coffee. What Starbucks didn't realise was just how strong that café culture truly was.

Australians didn't just drink coffee; they *lived* it. Local cafés were institutions—often family-run, fiercely independent and deeply attuned to the communities they served. They focused on quality over quantity and simplicity over spectacle.

Starbucks, however, entered with its full American playbook: oversized drinks with complex names (what the hell is a *venti*?), sweet flavourings unfamiliar to local palates, loyalty cards, branded mugs and stores that all looked and felt the same. Within a few short years, Starbucks had opened 87 stores around the country.

But instead of winning over coffee-loving Australians, Starbucks confused them. Many didn't understand the appeal — or the price tag. Flat whites gave way to *grandes*, and small, local charm was replaced with corporate sameness.

Rather than slow down and learn, Starbucks doubled down, adding *more* stores, *more* offerings, *more* frenzy. It assumed that what had worked elsewhere would work here too. But the more Starbucks tried to impose its model, the more resistance it encountered.

By 2008, the collapse was underway. Starbucks shut down 61 of its Australian stores in a single year, admitting defeat in a market it had utterly misunderstood.

This failure looked like a culture clash from the outside, but at its core was a lack of strategy. A failure to pause, observe and… *subtract*. Starbucks didn't take the time to ask: '*What can we remove? What doesn't belong here? What's already working that we shouldn't disrupt?*'

- It added when it should have taken away.
- It expanded when it should have refined.
- It assumed more would equal better.

What the market called for was *less*: fewer assumptions, fewer bells and whistles, less push and more listening.

It's easy to look back now and see where Starbucks went wrong but, at the time, every decision made sense to a company conditioned to equate scale with success. What it missed was that Australia didn't need a global coffee empire. It already had something better, and Starbucks, rather than clearing space to fit in, tried to build on top of these local successes.

- Imagine if it had started small with just a few stores, treating each as a listening post.

- Imagine if it had trimmed its menu, dropping the grandes, ventis and trentas and offering the language of the local café.

- Imagine if it had taken away everything that didn't support the Australian context and let the heart of the experience reveal itself.

Sadly for Starbucks, it didn't do any of these things, and as a result, it buried the very value it was trying to offer.

Our workplaces reward overwork, our economies prize growth at all costs, and our social circles admire those who seem to be doing the most. However, this belief is flawed.

More isn't always progress; sometimes it's the anchor that keeps us from moving at all.

THE 'MORE' REFLEX

We've been conditioned to believe that more is the answer:

- Feeling stuck? Add another meeting.

- Want to get promoted? Take on another project.

- Struggling to make sense of something? Read another book, join another group, download another app.

This reflex is a default setting that seems proactive, looks impressive and feels like progress, but it is rarely examined. More of what? For what purpose? At what cost?

This is the Red Brick of More: the instinct to add before we evaluate, accumulate before we clarify and act before we even decide if the action is required.

It shows up in boardrooms, at breakfast tables and in overstuffed strategies and overcomplicated systems, such as when we:

- Say yes when we mean maybe
- Download templates we'll never use
- Chase certifications, experiences or productivity hacks in the hope that this will be the thing that finally makes things click.

More is clever. It can be disguised as ambition, but it is often just noise with a reassuring pitch.

This red brick shows up:

- When we create a new team instead of fixing dysfunction in an existing one
- When we launch a new initiative without ending the last one
- When we keep layering on KPIs, platforms and dashboards that promise insight but only deliver overwhelm.

We equate 'more hours' with 'more commitment'. We think if we read more books, follow more experts and listen to more podcasts, we'll finally be ready to act. But 'more' doesn't always lead to a successful outcome. Sometimes it just gets in the way.

Red Brick Thinking begins the moment we notice the 'more impulse' and interrupt it.

WHY DO WE DEFAULT TO ACCUMULATION?

Starbucks's experience in Australia is a symptom of a broader cultural issue: the default to more is hardwired into human psychology. We hoard possessions, pack our schedules and cling to outdated processes because removing things feels like losing, while adding feels like progress.

As we already know, when people are asked to improve something, whether it's a business strategy, a product design or even a simple LEGO structure, their instinct is to add rather than subtract (addition bias).

It's because adding feels like action.

It gives us a quick hit of progress, so we feel useful, creative and in control. It looks like momentum and it feels like contribution, so we equate it with growth.

Subtraction, on the other hand, feels like risk.

It forces us to question what already exists. It asks us to let go of effort, of sunk costs, of ideas we once fought for, and that can feel uncomfortable, even threatening. This is especially true for fast-moving environments, where visibility matters and output is king, so adding is rewarded.

Subtraction is quieter; sometimes it looks like we're doing *nothing*.

But when we subtract well, we move with precision and can get closer to what matters.

> *That's the real shift Red Brick Thinking invites: to stop chasing the feeling of progress and start creating the conditions for actual progress.*

AMASSING HAS CONSEQUENCES

The more we take on, the busier we become, which fragments our focus and makes it harder to prioritise effectively.

This isn't only a business problem. It happens in our personal lives, too:

- We fill our homes with things we rarely use, convinced that having more will make life better. Storage unit rentals are at an all-time high, a testament to the fact that we have more than we can even fit in our own homes. Studies show that clutter increases stress and reduces our ability to focus.

- We overcommit to social events, activities and obligations, fearing that saying no means missing out. Yet burnout rates continue to rise, and many people report feeling stretched too thin.

- Our phones are overloaded with apps, our inboxes with emails and our minds with information. We consume content endlessly yet struggle to retain what truly matters. The more we try to keep up, the more overwhelmed we feel.

At a societal level, we glorify expansion: bigger houses, bigger salaries, bigger companies. Growth is seen as a measure of success, and yet history is full of examples where unchecked expansion led to collapse:

- The global fishing industry pushed harder, caught more and expanded endlessly, until the oceans began to empty. Nearly 90 per cent of the world's fish stocks are overexploited or depleted, devastating ecosystems and coastal economies. The relentless pursuit of *more* has left us with less.

- The fashion industry produces more clothing than ever before, yet landfills are overflowing with discarded garments. The constant drive for more has led to an unsustainable cycle of consumption and waste.

- Supermarkets are overflowing with food choices, restaurants serve portions too big to finish and households throw away uneaten meals. Globally, nearly a third of all the food produced is wasted, even as millions go hungry. More food hasn't resulted in better nutrition — just more waste.

These examples and many others demonstrate how overcommitting leads to stress, owning more leads to clutter and expanding too fast leads to instability.

WHEN ENOUGH STOPS FEELING LIKE ENOUGH

The Red Brick of More flatters. It tells you you're being productive, ambitious and diligent — that this next thing is the one that will finally make the difference. Left unchecked, it fills your life with activity and empties it of purpose.

- **You feel guilty doing nothing.** Stillness feels wasteful, so you reach for your phone at red lights and fill blank space in your calendar like it's a pothole. Even your weekends are scheduled. Downtime feels like wasted potential.

- **You say yes reflexively.** When requests come in, before you've even considered your capacity, your default answer is, 'Sure, I can fit that in.' You wear responsiveness like a badge of honour, but your yes is often someone else's priority, not yours.

- **You keep postponing the important for the urgent.** You're constantly in motion but rarely moving forward. The big, meaningful stuff sits untouched, while your days are consumed by smaller, quicker wins — things that feel good to tick off but don't actually shift the dial.

- **Your calendar is packed, but your priorities feel vague.** You're busy all day, yet when someone asks what you're working on, you hesitate. You've traded direction for density, and a full calendar has replaced a focused plan.

- **You're always on the verge of being ready.** You need one more article before you pitch, one more week before you start and one more draft before you share. You're constantly preparing, tweaking, perfecting, but not actually shipping.

- **You multitask like it's a sport.** You have two screens, five tabs open, half-written emails and a podcast playing while you answer messages during a meeting. You call it efficiency, but deep down, you know you're skimming through your day rather than really engaging with it.

- **You get annoyed at how busy you are but keep volunteering for more.** You vent about being overwhelmed — but the moment a new idea or request lands, you're in. There's a part of you that craves the fullness, even as it exhausts you.

- **You don't know what 'enough' looks like.** You can't define what *done* looks like. There's always more to read, to do, to improve. Satisfaction is elusive, and completion feels just out of reach.

- **You feel strangely tired but can't point to why.** There's no major crisis. Nothing's 'wrong', but there's a lingering state of fatigue. Your mind feels cluttered, and your focus feels fractured.

These are warning signs, and like every red brick, you can't shift what you refuse to see.

OUT WITH THE OLD

If we want to build sustainable businesses, productive workplaces and fulfilling lives, we need to shift from a mindset of accumulation to one of refinement. Instead of asking, *'What else can I add?'* we should be asking, *'What can I remove?'*

Dom Price, a Work Futurist at Atlassian, puts it simply: 'We never set out to make subtraction a thing. It just turned out that if we wanted to keep our best energy on what mattered, we had to get good at letting go.'

One of the ways Atlassian does this is through the 5Ls, a ritual that keeps teams honest without making their work heavy. They reflect on what they Loved, Laughed at, Loathed, Longed for and Learnt. It's way of making space for what's real, not just what's busy.

Dom laughs when he talks about it, but he's serious too. 'We even hold wakes for projects that need to end. If a team feels a lot of emotion about retiring a project, we don't pretend it didn't matter. We honour it. But we also make it really clear: here's what we're no longer focused on this year.'

Every year, Atlassian 'graduates' projects. This means shutting down, wrapping up and, in some cases, discontinuing projects that aren't doing what was intended. This is about intentionally reducing overload and actively making room for what's next (or for a new priority).

As Dom puts it, 'We're big fans of "Stop, Start, Continue." It's not about adding endlessly but being deliberate with our energy. If you don't stop things, you drown. Simple as that.'

Letting go of more is making sure the best of what you build actually has room to grow.

This same instinct plays out in our daily lives. Australians have long associated success with bigger homes — leading to higher mortgage debt, cluttered living spaces and a constant push for more — but a growing shift towards smaller, more intentional living, through the tiny house movement and minimalist lifestyles, challenges that mindset. People are downsizing possessions, cutting expenses and simplifying their daily routines. Instead of adding rooms, storage and possessions, they're removing excess and gaining freedom.

The irony is that the more we accumulate, the more distracted, overwhelmed and inefficient we become.

Meetings have become the default way of working, yet they rarely create the value they promise. A Microsoft study found that workers spend over half of their time communicating (in meetings, via emails and while working on collaborative tasks) and around 40 per cent of their time creating documents, spreadsheets and presentations, leaving little time for deep, meaningful work. Instead of solving problems, meetings often create new ones — diluting focus, extending workdays and increasing frustration. This is what led me to write my book *The 25 Minute Meeting* in 2018. Not only should we remove the red brick of too much time spent in meetings, but we also need to make them more impactful. Fewer, better meetings.

Tech companies, including Atlassian and Shopify, have begun cutting unnecessary meetings altogether, freeing employees to focus on actual work rather than endless discussions about work. The real question isn't 'Should this be a meeting?' but 'Does this need to exist at all?'

To-do lists, once seen as productivity tools, often create more stress than they solve. Studies show that only 41 per cent of tasks on a to-do list ever get completed. The rest linger, creating mental clutter that drains energy and fuels a sense of inadequacy.

The problem isn't the list itself; it's the assumption that everything written down is equally important. Instead of accumulating an endless backlog, focus only on what truly needs doing today. By reducing the list, you increase the likelihood of finishing it and finishing well.

The second book in my It's About Time series, *The First 2 Hours*, dealt with the opportunity to pay attention to the clock in your body, not the one on the wall. In essence, *when* you do something is at least as important as *what* you are doing. When we carve up our to-do list according to the best time of day to do things, we can get through our list as well as maintain our energy levels.

Burnout is no longer just a personal issue; it's a recognised workplace crisis. It's about the sheer cognitive overload of switching between tasks, constantly being available and never feeling like you've done enough.

Forward-thinking companies are starting to take burnout seriously, shifting away from hustle culture and toward smarter, more sustainable ways of working. The most productive people aren't the ones who push the hardest — they're the ones who know when to step back.

Starbucks chased growth at all costs and paid the price. Many of us do the same: taking on more than we can handle, saying yes out of obligation and mistaking busyness for progress.

The good news is that breaking free from the *more* mentality doesn't require a massive overhaul. It starts with small but powerful shifts in thinking.

THE COURAGE TO CUT

When you've built your identity on being capable, resourceful and always up for more, subtraction feels like surrender.

The Red Brick of More isn't just about doing too much. It's about believing that more is where the value is: more tools, goals, learning… more everything.

So, when the time comes to remove something — to stop doing, to stop chasing — the fear creeps in:

- Will I fall behind?

- Will people think I've lost my edge?

- What if this thing I stop doing turns out to be the one that mattered most?

This is the emotional cost of subtraction. We don't just remove tasks; we challenge the stories that say *doing more* is the same as *being more*.

More isn't always better, sometimes it's just… more.

Removing the Red Brick of More is about discernment.

Start small. You don't need to torch your to-do list or flee to the hills. Pick one area — your week, your workload, your digital clutter — and look for the excess. Look for the bulging that once made sense but now just fills space.

Letting go of more often means confronting an old story that says your worth is measured by how much you carry. It's a story that says stopping is a risk, but adding is safe.

When you start editing your commitments, your responsibilities, your inputs — not out of guilt, but out of focus — something changes. The din softens, the signal sharpens, and what remains is what matters.

Dare I say it, you'll become *more* effective, *more* respected and *more* fulfilled, all by doing less.

Chapter 5

Hustle

For decades, Nick Cave built a reputation as one of Australia's most intense and prolific artists. His work, whether with the Bad Seeds or on film scores and novels, has always pulsed with emotional weight and dark beauty. But in 2015, Cave's life was shattered when his 15-year-old son, Arthur, died in a tragic accident. It was the kind of loss that changes everything, and it brought Cave's creative momentum to a full stop.

While many artists might have buried themselves in work to cope, Cave did something radical: he stepped away.

He didn't rush to create or force the words. He simply stopped. He allowed silence, grief and space to take the place of his usual relentless output. There were no deadlines or expectations, just time.

And then, slowly and quietly, something emerged.

In 2019, Nick Cave and the Bad Seeds released *Ghosteen*, an album that critics have called the band's most transcendent work. It's sparse, ethereal and achingly vulnerable — unlike anything they'd produced before.

Cave described the process as 'amassing a stockpile of lines and thoughts, images and ideas.' He wasn't crafting or constructing the songs in his usual way. Instead, he was receiving them, letting them come through.

Cave's experience echoes the principles of deep listening, a practice championed by bestselling author and award-winning podcaster Oscar Trimboli. Trimboli teaches that true listening goes beyond words. It's about creating space, noticing what's not said and tuning into silence as much as sound.

I was speaking with Oscar about the role of silence in how we work and lead. I admitted that for me, and for many of us raised in Western systems, silence still feels like something to avoid. It's uncomfortable, awkward and a space we're supposed to fill.

Oscar gently challenged that. He explained that in many high-context cultures, including Aboriginal communities in Australia, silence holds a different kind of power. It's a sign of wisdom and a mark of respect. 'Silence,' he said, 'carries authority.'

This stayed with me.

He went on to explain how silence shortens meetings, reduces misunderstandings and creates space for what actually matters. 'When we're not rushing to respond or compete for airtime, something shifts. People stop saying what they think they should say and start saying what they truly mean.'

Silence is intentional, inviting depth. In a world that rewards speed, silence is a kind of revolution that leads to better listening, lighter leadership and more meaningful impact.

In Cave's surrender to grief and stillness, he became a vessel rather than a creator. He wasn't filling the space; he was receiving what emerged from it. This is deep listening at its most profound: not striving to be heard, but preparing to hear fully, deeply, without an agenda. It's a reminder that insight often arrives when we stop trying to produce and start making space to receive.

Most of us, when stuck or overwhelmed, double down by adding more effort, inputs and noise. Cave's story reminds us of a deeper truth. Sometimes the only way forward is to stop: to remove the expectation, step back from the pressure and let space, not struggle, lead the way.

Breakthroughs don't always arise from force. Often, they are a result of silence.

PRODUCTIVITY'S FAVOURITE LIE

The Red Brick of Hustle is the belief that if we're not pushing, grinding or filling every spare moment with output, we're not being productive.

It doesn't just shape what we do — it shapes who we believe we are.

I'm the only person in my extended family who runs their own business. When I visit them or pick up the phone for a catch-up, someone inevitably asks, 'How's work? Are you busy?'

This well-meaning question reveals that in our culture, *busyness* still carries weight. It's shorthand for doing well, being in demand and staying relevant. If you're busy, things must be going great.

It's taken me years to unlearn that idea.

For a long time, I wore busy like an emblem of success. I'd rattle off how many workshops I was running, how many projects were on the go, how many nights I'd been on the road and how many months in advance I was booked out. The more I stacked my calendar, the more legitimate I felt: if I was exhausted, I must be succeeding.

Somewhere along the way, I stopped finding pride in that answer. 'Busy' started to feel like a cover story and a way to avoid talking about what really mattered. It was movement without meaning.

Now, when my family asks, 'Are you busy?' I smile and say, 'I have enough.'

It throws them for a second … and then we move on. But I like that little pause. It's a moment where I don't automatically reach for 'busy' to validate how things are going.

These days, I don't want a full calendar. I want one that has adaptive capacity — space to think, breathe and take on a new and interesting project if it comes up. I don't want to be the 'I'm sorry, I'm booked out for six months' person anymore: not so I can do nothing, but so I can do the *right* things.

Hustle has become more than a way of working. It's become a kind of modern-day virtue — a marker of ambition, seriousness and drive. We wear it as a status symbol:

- Always busy
- Always available
- Always chasing the next thing.

At its core, hustle promises control. Keep moving and nothing can catch you. Keep producing and you'll stay ahead. It tells us that speed equals relevance, and that rest is for those who haven't yet figured out how to get ahead. It leaves us feeling as if slowing down is a sign of spinning wheels, and pausing is a risk to our reputation.

You see it in the language we use:

- Rise and grind.

- Sleep when you're dead.

- No days off.

Elon Musk famously said, 'Nobody ever changed the world on 40 hours a week.' He followed up by suggesting that 80 hours a week was a good target.

I'm not sure fellow gazillionaire Warren Buffett would agree. He's famous not for grinding 80-hour weeks, but for guarding his time like treasure and creating massive value through focus and restraint. He spends most of his workday reading, thinking and *doing* very little, by traditional productivity standards. As he's said many times, 'I insist on a lot of time being spent, almost every day, to just sit and think.'

As one of Australia's most values-driven and successful social enterprises, Thankyou has flipped the fast-moving consumer goods industry on its head. Its mission is to end global poverty by redirecting profits from everyday products — such as water, body wash, nappies — towards life-changing projects around the world.

But unlike many high-growth startups, Thankyou didn't rise on the back of 80-hour weeks, burnout culture or blitz-scaling.

At the height of Thankyou's rise, the pressure to grow was intense and constant. The team could feel it from all sides: more product lines, more markets, more media. On paper, this was success — but inside the business, the cracks were showing.

Daniel Flynn, co-founder of Thankyou, described it to me as a weight they could physically feel. 'We saw what it was doing to our families, our relationships, our team. Even the vision itself began to fray at the edges.'

Growth had always been the goal, but they'd reached a point where the pace was compromising the foundation. 'We didn't want to build something that looked good on the outside but would collapse under pressure. That's not what Thankyou was ever meant to be.'

When hustle is equated with heroism, slowing down can feel almost subversive. But that's exactly what Daniel and the team chose to do. 'We had to hit the brakes. Not because we weren't ambitious, but because we finally saw the cost.'

That decision didn't come easily. It required a shift in mindset, from building an empire to nurturing an ecosystem. 'We started seeing Thankyou less as a single brand doing everything, and more as a movement powered by partnerships. That meant letting go of control. It meant saying no more than we said yes.'

The hardest part was turning down good things like speaking gigs, deals and ideas that sounded exciting but pulled focus. 'One of our mentors said, "Every time you say yes to something, you're saying no to something else." We started treating "yes" like a precious resource.'

Daniel tells a story that's become something of a guiding metaphor for their approach: 'To lead the orchestra, you have to be willing to turn your back to the crowd.' It's not always popular and it doesn't always make sense to outsiders, but it's how they've stayed aligned to what matters most.

Thankyou is proof that you can have an impact at 40 hours a week, if you spend those hours wisely.

HUSTLE HAS BECOME THE DEFAULT MODE

It starts small, with a bit of after-hours work, a weekend catch-up, and a calendar that's tight but manageable — until suddenly, you can't remember the last time you finished something without already thinking about the next thing.

Perhaps, most insidiously, hustle often feels like progress, like you're doing it right — until you stop and realise you haven't had a clear thought, a deep breath or a day off in weeks.

The Red Brick of Hustle convinces us that our worth is earned by how much we do, that value comes from volume, that rest is a luxury and that stillness is suspect.

Hustle doesn't always lead to impact. More often, it leads to burnout disguised as productivity.

This brick is substantial, and it's everywhere.

ALWAYS DOING ISN'T ALWAYS WINNING

Exhaustion is worn like a symbol of success, and hustle has become a lifestyle brand. You'll find it on coffee mugs and Instagram bios. The unspoken mantra tells us that if you're not pushing, grinding or doing more, you're falling behind.

Underneath the energy drinks and late-night emails is a quieter truth: we've confused effort with effectiveness, and we're paying the price.

Psychologists call it the *effort heuristic* — the idea that the harder something is, the more valuable it must be. It's why we glorify the founder pulling 100-hour weeks and quietly shame the parent who logs off at 5pm, and it's why we fill our calendars with meetings that don't need to happen, answer emails at midnight and treat rest like a luxury instead of a tool.

In 2014, researchers at Stanford University found that productivity drops sharply once people exceed 50 hours of work per week. At 55 hours, it falls off a cliff. After 70 hours, the extra time produces no additional results, just fatigue.

Still, many industries keep pushing. For years, Australia's mining sector had a culture of longer shifts, higher output. Workers routinely clocked 12-hour days, six or seven days in a row. The logic seemed solid — more time, more tonnes — but the data told a different story.

Cognitive performance declined and mistakes increased, while some workers, nearing the end of their shifts, were functionally impaired to the level of legal intoxication. Fatigue-related accidents rose, and some had tragic consequences.

Eventually, even the biggest operators had to listen. Companies like BHP and Rio Tinto began introducing fatigue-management programs: capped hours, mandatory rest, smarter rosters. What they got was fewer incidents, better retention and higher-quality output.

Doing less didn't hurt the bottom line — it protected it.

When leaders burn out, it doesn't just affect them; it infects the system beneath them, because overwork spills and decision-making and creativity suffer. Brilliance rarely emerges from burnout — it emerges from space.

Some of the world's best ideas weren't born in 2am meetings or multitasking marathons. They emerged on walks, in silence and during sabbaticals. They came when the brain was resting.

- **Einstein's thought walks.** Albert Einstein famously took long, slow walks, sometimes for hours, during which he would let his mind wander. He called these his 'combinatory play' moments, when ideas from different domains collided in unexpected ways. The theory of relativity wasn't only the result of scientific lab work. It also needed deep, untethered reflection. He was not attached to any particular solution; instead, he allowed one to emerge.

- **Bill Gates's 'think weeks'.** Twice a year, Bill Gates retreats into seclusion for a week. No meetings, no tech interruptions — just books, notes and silence. Many of Microsoft's major product shifts and philanthropic strategies have been shaped during these periods. The space to think without reacting is where Gates connects dots that daily busyness would otherwise obscure.

- **Lin-Manuel Miranda and the New York subway.** The spark for the musical *Hamilton* didn't come from a writing session or a creative sprint, it came during a break. While on holiday from his first Broadway show (*In the Heights*), Miranda picked up Ron Chernow's biography of Alexander Hamilton to read for fun. Later, riding alone on the New York subway, he found himself free-associating lines and rhythms in his head. No agenda or deadline — just rhythm, movement and mental space. That quiet commute laid the foundation for what would become a cultural phenomenon.

BURN BRIGHT, BURN FAST

At first, hustle feels invigorating. There's a rush that comes with being the one who's always on, always moving, always producing. People admire your energy and you're praised for your responsiveness, work ethic and results.

But hustle has a hidden toll, and it rarely sends you a bill until it's already too late.

The cost isn't just burnout in the dramatic, collapse-on-the-bathroom-floor sense (though for some, that's exactly where it ends up). Often, the cost is quieter and more cumulative. It builds, unnoticed, until suddenly you realise your days are packed but your work feels shallow:

- You're busy but not fulfilled.

- You're producing but not thinking.

- You're getting things done but struggling to remember why they matter.

When you're constantly in motion, you lose access to the perspective that only comes from stillness. Creative ideas dry up, strategic thinking becomes harder and you stop asking the bigger questions because you're too busy answering the urgent ones.

Hustle erodes your depth.

And then there's the emotional tax:

- The tension that builds in your body

- The resentment that creeps in around the edges

- The relationships that slip, slowly, because you're never fully present

- The creeping feeling that you're living your life on fast forward and missing the actual movie.

In workplaces, hustle is rewarded until the team burns out, mistakes start creeping in and the creative well runs dry, with no one knowing how to refill it. All that surface activity starts to come undone, because hustle isn't scalable. It's a short-term strategy disguised as long-term dedication.

Most tragically, hustle teaches us to ignore our inner signals: the tiredness, the tension, the gut instinct to pause. We override them all and push through, because hustle tricks us into believing that being busy is the same as being effective and that output is the same as impact. There is a difference, though, and by the time we feel it, the cost has already compounded.

Ironically, the most productive countries don't hustle like we do. Denmark, the Netherlands and Norway have shorter work weeks, encourage deep rest, have consistently higher productivity and champion innovation and wellbeing.

Meanwhile, Japan, once the model of a strong work ethic, is grappling with a national crisis. There is even a word for it — *karoshi*. Horrifyingly, it means death from overwork.

WHEN HUSTLE BECOMES HABIT

Hustle builds gradually, until busyness feels like your natural state and exhaustion becomes background noise. This isn't sustainable, and it isn't smart.

The danger lies in how normal it starts to feel and how easy it is to confuse constant motion with meaningful progress.

- **You recognise it in the moments between the meetings, in the space you no longer give yourself.** It shows in the reflex to open your laptop on a Sunday night just to 'get ahead', in the urge to check emails in the waiting room or when you feel anxious if your calendar isn't full. You may brag about being flat out, like it's impressive.

- **You notice that rest makes you edgy.** You don't know how to sit still without reaching for your phone. Slowing down feels unsafe, like something might fall apart if you stop.

- **Your mornings start with a sprint, not reflection.** Your focus jumps from one task to the next, without finishing any of them properly. You can't remember the last time you did deep work without interruption, or without checking Slack, Teams or your inbox mid-thought.

- **You feel a subtle shift in how you talk.** You say things like 'I'm slammed', 'I just need to get through this week' or 'I'll rest after this deadline', even though you said the same thing last week.

Maybe you're productive but you're also perpetually tired and, somewhere underneath all that output, there's a quiet question you've stopped asking: 'Is this working?'

If that question stings, pay attention. Hustle is no longer helping you move forward; it's keeping you too busy to notice you're stuck.

SLOWING DOWN WITHOUT LOSING YOUR EDGE

Removing the Red Brick of Hustle seldom means letting go of ambition. It means choosing a different pace that allows room for depth, reflection and direction.

For many of us, hustle has become a kind of insurance policy.

- Keep going, and you'll stay ahead.
- Keep busy, and no one can accuse you of slacking.

But that pace comes at a cost to your thinking, your health and your ability to do your best work. Slowing down is an opportunity for recalibration.

If you find yourself reaching for the next task out of habit, pause and ask yourself, 'Am I doing this because it's useful, or because I'm uncomfortable not doing it?'

Letting go of hustle is about trusting that rest, reflection and white space are not indulgent; instead, they're strategic. They allow your work to breathe, and they allow *you* to breathe.

You don't need to prove your worth through exhaustion or stay in motion to stay relevant. Often the people who make the biggest impact aren't the busiest; they're the clearest.

So, reclaim your thinking and honour your energy. Real momentum comes from direction, not speed.

And if it feels strange to slow down, that's a sign you're finally doing it differently.

Chapter 6

Someday

Winning the lottery is often seen as the ultimate dream: instant wealth, total freedom and a lifetime of luxury.

But for many, the reality is far different. Sometimes, lottery winners end up worse off than before they won. Their relationships break down, they make reckless investments, and in extreme cases, they find themselves bankrupt.

- William 'Bud' Post won $16.2 million in the Pennsylvania Lottery in 1988. Within weeks, he had spent a fortune on extravagant purchases, including a twin-engine airplane, despite not having a pilot's license. His brother attempted to have him murdered for the inheritance, and an ex-girlfriend successfully sued him for a share of his winnings. By the end of his life, Post was over $1 million in debt and relied on food stamps.

- Evelyn Adams won the New Jersey Lottery not once, but twice, in 1985 and 1986, totalling $5.4 million. However, her compulsive gambling habits led her to squander her fortune at Atlantic City casinos and through failed business ventures. Eventually, she lost everything and was reported to be living in a caravan.

- Michael Carroll, a 19-year-old garbage collector from the UK, won £9.7 million in the National Lottery in 2002. He quickly became infamous for his lavish lifestyle, spending his fortune on drugs, parties, cars and generous handouts to friends and family. Within a few years, Carroll was bankrupt and had returned to his previous job as a rubbish collector.

- Janite Lee won an $18 million jackpot in the Illinois Lottery in 1993 and generously donated to political and charitable causes. However, within a decade, her spending outpaced her wealth, leading to bankruptcy.

It should be the ultimate shortcut to happiness: a winning ticket, a life reset, no more bills, no more stress, just possibility. But for many lottery winners, the dream quickly collapses under its own weight — not because they're reckless or ungrateful, but because sudden abundance almost never comes with instructions.

Sudden influxes of money rarely erase problems; instead, they will likely amplify them.

- What was once a quiet habit becomes a full-blown problem.

- A vague insecurity becomes a loud panic.

- The pressure to make good decisions, be generous and prove you're not wasting the money becomes a full-time job.

Friends turn distant, family members become expectant, the spotlight shines ... and not everyone likes what it reveals.

Without a strong sense of purpose, it's easy to lose your footing. Many lottery winners fall into a pattern that looks, from the outside, like indulgence, but inside feels more like grasping. They make extravagant purchases, enter rushed investments and are impulsively generous — not because they're careless, but because no one ever taught them how to hold that much power. Without anchors, clear values, honest relationships and meaningful goals, the wealth drifts. And so do they.

What should simplify life ends up complicating it.

ARE WE THERE YET?

This trap is not just for the newly rich, but for anyone who's ever said, 'When I finally get there, everything will be different.'

We pin our hopes to future milestones — a house, a title, a big break or the next level — convinced that fulfilment is just around the corner. We chase it, thinking it will fix what today cannot; instead, it distracts us even more.

This is the Red Brick of Someday: the illusion that one more thing will finally be *the* thing, and happiness lives just past the next milestone. But 'someday' has no finish line.

Freedom means stepping off the ladder, even if you haven't reached the top yet.

THE HEDONIC TREADMILL

The *hedonic treadmill* is our natural tendency to return to a baseline level of happiness, no matter what happens.

Buy a new car, get a promotion, move into a dream home. Each brings a rush of excitement, but before long, life normalises and we start craving the next big thing. The thrill fades, and the search begins again.

We tell ourselves just one more step, one more achievement, one more purchase, and then I'll be happy.

And for a moment, it works. You feel the glow of achievement, the thrill of possession, the brief high of 'I did it.' But then the glow fades: the house needs repairs, the car becomes just another ride and the job, once a dream, becomes another source of stress.

So we reach for the next milestone, the next title, the next thing.

Psychologists Philip Brickman and Donald Campbell first named this cycle in 1971. One of their most striking studies compared two wildly different life events: winning the lottery and becoming paraplegic. You might assume the outcomes would be opposite. But within a year, both groups had returned to roughly the same level of happiness they'd felt before. The conclusion was unsettling: even extraordinary events, fortune or upheaval, don't change our emotional baseline for long.

This adaptation trickles into everyday life:

- Get a raise, and you feel richer — until your lifestyle inflates.

- Hit a social media milestone, and you celebrate — until the next goal appears.

- Launch a successful product, and you're proud — until competitors catch up.

The bar keeps moving, and we keep running.

Marketers don't just sell products, they sell dissatisfaction. Not directly, but subtly: 'You're not quite complete,' they murmur. 'You could be better, more radiant, more productive, more secure.' The fix is only one purchase away.

They craft a gap between who you are and who you could be and then offer to fill it: a new phone, a new serum, a new streaming series queued to autoplay so there's no pause between episodes. Everything is designed to keep you leaning forward and chasing: never resting, not quite satisfied and certainly not done.

The wellness industry does it too, with one more supplement, one more cold plunge and one more 'morning routine that changed my life'. Fitness programs sell transformation as a subscription model, not a destination.

At a societal level, we've built entire economies on this loop. GDP must grow, companies must scale and success must compound. Economist Richard Easterlin, however, found something odd: as national wealth increased, happiness didn't. More money didn't mean more wellbeing, it just meant … more.

That's the trap of the treadmill: you're moving, but you're not arriving.

Satisfaction almost never scales the way status does. It's not in the next version or the next title; it lives in your ability to stop long enough to appreciate what you already have.

THE DISTANCE THAT NEVER CLOSES

The Red Brick of Someday is subtle, but its cost is steep. It won't burn you out in the way hustle does or overload your schedule like complexity or overcommitment. Instead, it robs you of something far more personal: your presence.

Someday stretches life into a permanent holding pattern:

- You're living near your life, but never quite in it.

- You're working towards a version of yourself that will finally be worthy of peace, rest and satisfaction.

- You'll slow down when the project finishes, when the kids are older or when the savings hit that magic number.

Until then, you keep going, deferring and waiting.

And ever so quietly, joy becomes conditional, fulfilment becomes a moving target and every success gets rerouted into the next goalpost. You can't celebrate because you're already behind on the next thing.

In your mind, life will begin when...

- things calm down.

- you've earned it.

- you feel ready.

But that moment is always *just* out of reach, like chasing the horizon. No matter how fast you move, it keeps moving too.

The emotional toll builds slowly via restlessness, low-grade discontent and a sense that no matter what you do, it's never quite enough. You might look successful on the outside — goals hit, boxes ticked — but inside, there's a sense of suspension. Of *not quite yet.*

This way of thinking also changes how we relate to others. You might find yourself distracted in conversations, frustrated that things aren't moving faster or avoiding real joy because it feels unearned.

We don't just delay contentment; we delay connection.

In organisations, the cost is strategic as well as emotional. When leaders operate in someday mode, they're constantly chasing bigger, newer and more, without recognising the value of what's already working. They miss the moment and so do their teams.

> *The real tragedy of someday isn't that we don't get what we want: it's that we miss what we already have.*

And all the while, life is happening on the sidelines, waiting for us to notice.

LIVING IN THE WAITING ROOM

The Red Brick of Someday is not shouty. It often feels like a constant undertone: a quiet belief that life isn't quite ready to be enjoyed just yet.

- **You hear it in the quiet bargain you make with yourself ('I'll feel better when … ').** When the project's done, when the next school term starts, when the bonus arrives. But the 'when' keeps shifting. Relief never arrives, because the goalposts are always moving — and you're the one moving them.

- **You notice it after a big win.** The presentation lands, the deal closes, the thing you worked so hard for gets ticked off… and within hours, maybe minutes, it fades. The satisfaction dissolves, and instead of celebrating, you're scanning for what's next as if the goal was only ever a placeholder.

- **You find yourself shelving joy like it's a luxury you haven't earned yet.** The good wine stays unopened; the long weekend never gets booked. You keep telling yourself you'll enjoy these things later, when things settle down. But later never arrives, and joy becomes a reward you never quite feel entitled to claim.

- **You catch yourself outsourcing too much to 'future you'.** Future you is the version of you who will have more time or energy — the one who'll finally get organised, start the good habit or fix the mess. But 'today you' keeps adding to the list while quietly hoping that future you will be better at boundaries.

- **You feel oddly distant from the life you've built.** People call you successful, but it barely lands. You look at your calendar, résumé and LinkedIn profile and wonder who it really belongs to. You feel as if you've climbed a ladder, but it's leaning against the wrong wall.

- **You spend more time fantasising about a turning point than actually planning one.** You imagine the moment it all clicks — the job that changes everything, the phone call, the pivot, the breakthrough. It's a comforting but dangerous image because while you wait for the turning point to arrive, the life you want stays on hold.

Sometimes it sounds like ambition and sometimes it sounds like discipline, but the Red Brick of Someday is actually underpinned by uncertainty: a fear of being content, in case it means you've stopped growing.

The hardest part is that 'someday' feels like preparation, as if you're being responsible and smart. Until one day you look up and realise you've built a life that's always waiting to begin.

GOOD ENOUGH

Studies show that gratitude can disrupt the treadmill effect. We don't necessarily need to journal about gratitude or follow a perfect method; it can be as simple as taking a moment to deliberately pause to say, 'This is good.' Focusing on experiences over possessions also helps. We remember moments, not objects. The memory of a birthday dinner is stronger than the memory of the shoes we wore that evening.

Oliver Burkeman, in his book *Four Thousand Weeks*, says our obsession with optimisation is robbing us of joy. Life is finite and time is non-refundable, so embracing that limitation, rather than trying to hack it, is the path to peace.

Daniel Pink, in his book *Drive*, draws the same line from another angle. He shows how intrinsic motivation, autonomy, mastery and purpose create deeper, longer-lasting fulfilment than anything external ever could.

What if the boldest thing you could say in a culture obsessed with more is, 'I'm good enough'? It's not a sign you've given up or you're settling for less; instead, it demonstrates you've stopped waiting to feel whole. You've noticed the arrival, not just the goal.

A friend's daughter, Taylor, had what many would call a good thing going. At 28, she was climbing the workplace ladder, earning solid money and ticking all the boxes that hustle culture laid out for her.

But something didn't feel right. The long commute and the rigid structure led to the quiet sense that she was working harder than she needed to, for things she didn't actually want.

So, she made what some would see as a bold move and what others would call madness. She took a 20 per cent pay cut in exchange for one thing: agency.

No more peak-hour rush, and no more desk for desk's sake. She now works from home full-time, saving hours each week and spending them on the things that matter: her wellbeing, her family and her life.

Taylor is part of a growing wave of Millennials and Generation Zs who are saying no — not to work, but to *overwork*. They're opting out of the 'always-on' mentality that has defined previous generations. They're choosing boundaries over burnout, flexibility over frenzy, and enough over endless.

They're not quitting. They're just done chasing someone else's version of success.

For many of them, they no longer focus on climbing ladders just to reach the top; instead, they want to reach a point and realise, 'This is enough.'

The hedonic treadmill will always be there, whirring softly beneath the surface, but you don't have to keep running. You can step off, look around and start moving forward — not necessarily towards the *next* thing, but into the life you already have.

And that changes everything.

TRADE THE HORIZON FOR WHAT'S HERE

Letting go of the Red Brick of Someday means learning to live with your desires, without letting them defer your joy.

Start by noticing where you've hit pause on your life. What have you told yourself you can't feel, do or enjoy until something else happens? Is it the dream home? The next career step? The final piece of debt being paid off?

Bring moments forward without waiting for the perfect time:

- Use the nice candle on a Tuesday.
- Make that meal you're saving for guests.
- Wear the outfit you said was for special occasions.

Life is *the occasion.*

This means de-coupling your identity from outcomes. Let the big dreams stay in view — but hold them lightly. They can inspire, but they don't need to delay your peace.

You don't need to wait to achieve a milestone to feel grounded, proud or whole. You can practise those emotions now and, ironically, when you do, the chase often softens. You begin moving from fullness, not lack.

Letting go of the Red Brick of Someday starts by grounding your vision in what's already within reach, because the life you're waiting for is already happening right here, in this moment.

YOU'VE ARRIVED

My friend and fellow author Gabrielle Dolan recently drew a line in the sand. After decades in corporate banking, a string of bestselling books and a speaking career that's taken her everywhere from Harvard to events alongside Barack Obama, she hit pause. A health scare in 2025 shook things up, forcing her to ask a bigger question: 'What does success really mean now?'

Over cocktails, she put it plainly: 'I started to think maybe this was my wake-up call. That maybe enough really is enough. Why was I still chasing more money or work?'

We laughed about how easy it is to let targets, book sales, gigs and revenue sneak in and take over. We realised that sometimes ego slips in and starts steering the wheel, long after impact has taken the back seat.

Gabrielle has since scaled back her commitments dramatically. She's trimmed her overheads, rebalanced her time and discovered that what looked like a 'loss' on paper barely registered in real life. Instead, she gained something more valuable: space for family, freedom and a lot more golf.

Recognising 'enough' is a profound act of awareness, because when you stop chasing what's next, you can finally see what's here in the present.

That shift creates room for:

- **Better choices.** When you're not operating from scarcity or FOMO (fear of missing out), decisions become cleaner. You're not reacting; you're responding with purpose.

- **Deeper satisfaction.** Constant pursuit breeds dissatisfaction. When you pause to recognise what's already working and what's already meaningful, contentment deepens.

- **Real freedom.** The most exhausting part of modern life is the belief that we should always be doing more. 'Enough' untethers you from that.

Imagine what your life, your leadership and your creativity could look like if you weren't trying to outrun the next milestone. Instead of striving to accumulate, focus on refining. And instead of measuring success by what you've added, define it by what you've intentionally let go of.

Contentment is an underrated state. Imagine for a moment being fully content with your lot in life — having the quiet confidence of knowing you don't need another win to feel whole. You can appreciate where you are even as you keep moving forward.

Contentment allows you to enjoy the view from halfway up the mountain, not just from the summit.

A study published in *The Journal of Positive Psychology* found that people who regularly practised gratitude and contentment reported significantly higher levels of life satisfaction. They paid attention to what they already had rather than striving for more, and that attention became a form of nourishment.

The idea that happiness comes after success is backwards. Shawn Achor, in his book *The Happiness Advantage*, flips the equation. His research shows that happiness isn't the reward for hard work — it's the fuel. People who start from appreciation tend to be more productive, more resilient and more creative.

STOP POSTPONING YOUR LIFE

We are masters of the delayed arrival. We tell ourselves the good life is just over the next hill: that once we've achieved more, earned more, fixed more, then we'll feel the way we want to feel.

But someday is a moving target. The more we chase it, the further it drifts.

Letting go of someday is the beginning of presence. It's choosing to live fully now, even as you work towards what's next. It's realising that contentment and progress are not mutually exclusive.

Choose to live like this moment counts — because it does.

You don't need to wait for the world to tell you you've made it.

You get to decide, and maybe the right thing to do in a culture of endless pursuit is to stop chasing.

Chapter 7

Accumulation

It starts before sunrise.

A line of shoppers snakes around the corner of a suburban shopping centre, bleary-eyed but determined. Some sip takeaway coffee, while others bounce on the balls of their feet, ready to sprint. It's Boxing Day, the unofficial holiday for buying things we didn't know we needed.

The clock strikes 9am, doors slide open, the mood shifts and what was a queue becomes a crush as people flood in like it's a race — elbows out, eyes fixed. A woman dives for a flatscreen, teenagers argue over the last air fryer and trolleys overflow with 'bargains', from half-price blenders and stackable storage to novelty socks and a juicer someone's uncle might appreciate.

By noon, the car park is gridlocked, the boot won't close and the excitement is fading.

In 2024, Australians spent $1.3 billion on Boxing Day sales. Over one billion dollars in one day. Not on emergencies or essentials, but on stuff. Most of it bought in a rush, wrapped in the logic of 'too good to pass up' and destined for a dark cupboard, a regift pile or landfill within six weeks.

We are drowning in possessions, and we call it lifestyle:

- We're not hoarders, we're 'home organisers'.
- We're not overconsuming, we're 'treating ourselves'.

But the reality is harder to hashtag, with the average home containing over 300 000 individual items. Consumption gone crazy.

Australians are overwhelmed by their own abundance, with nearly half admitting they own too much stuff and one in five saying they simply don't have enough space at home.

The worst part is that we hardly notice anymore. We've normalised drowning in drawers that won't close, garages that don't fit cars and subscriptions we forgot we had, along with the quiet anxiety of wondering where all our space and time has gone.

As Chuck Palahniuk describes in his novel *Fight Club*, 'Advertising has these people chasing cars and clothes they don't need. Generations have been working in jobs they hate, just so they can buy what they don't really need.'

Accumulating stuff we don't need is one part of the problem, but what is this stuff costing us?

A CULTURE ADDICTED TO ACCUMULATION

We didn't get here by accident.

For decades, we've been quietly trained to believe that success can be measured in square metres, handbag brands and how many boxes we need when we move.

We don't just live in a growth economy, we perform it: bigger houses, newer cars, newer phones (even when last year's model works perfectly), seasonal wardrobes, shoe towers, tech upgrades and kitchen gadgets that do one job.

We don't ask if we need it. We ask, 'Why not?'

Advertising sells us the story that happiness is something you can purchase, identity is something you can curate, status is visible and meaning comes with packaging. It's all around us in the language we now use without thinking:

- 'Retail therapy' because shopping is positioned as self-care

- 'Treat yourself' because restraint is outdated

- 'Must-have' because not having it means you're missing something essential.

We call it commerce, when actually it's conditioning.

We're lured in by scarcity language ('limited time only!'), baited with promises of instant rewards ('flash sale!') and hooked by aspirational branding — images of someone calmer, cooler and more stylish than we feel.

We're told, explicitly or otherwise, that buying something will close the gap between who we are and who we want to be.

It's psychological.

Every item we bring into our lives carries a story, a promise, a projection:

- The shirt that's not just cotton? It also represents who you thought you'd be when you wore it.

- That pile of unread books? It also represents who you hoped you'd become.

- The juicer? The treadmill? The ring light? They're not just objects; they're little totems of potential.

We link our belongings to our identity. According to the *extended self theory,* the things we own aren't just things — they're extensions of who we are. That worn-out hoodie, that old university mug, the crafting supplies for a long-forgotten hobby ... they tell our story, even when they're no longer serving us.

Shopping is a rush. Buying and acquiring things lights up our brain's reward centres, so what we think of as retail therapy is actually our biology at work. However, the hit is short-lived, and what lingers is the overflow — the clutter in our lives.

Clutter is often emotional insulation, with studies showing links between clutter and anxiety, decision fatigue and even depression. When life feels out of control, we hold on to stuff as a kind of armour.

We don't just clutter our homes, we clutter our sense of self — and because we rarely stop to audit any of it, we confuse *having* with *being*. We collect, store, display and upgrade not out of deep desire, but out of habit: the quiet, gnawing fear that doing less or wanting less means *being* less.

But what if it's the opposite? What if letting go of our unnecessary, outdated or aspirational clutter isn't loss, but liberation?

What if clearing the physical makes way for the psychological?

That's what Red Brick Thinking asks of us: how can we carry less and free up space?

FROM FULL CUPBOARDS TO FULL CALENDARS

Clutter starts with things, but it rarely stops there. It spreads to your calendar, your inbox, your headspace.

The same impulse that drives us to fill our cupboards also drives us to fill our time. We over-schedule, over-promise and over-extend:

- We treat every invitation like an obligation.

- We stack meetings back to back and call it productivity.

- We fill gaps in our days with scrolling, swiping and replying, not because it nourishes us but because emptiness now feels uncomfortable.

Stillness feels suspect.

We've been conditioned to associate space with laziness or boredom, as if a blank slot in the calendar means we're slacking, or white space on our desks or in our wardrobes is a sign we're not trying hard enough. We don't just have cluttered homes; we have cluttered lives.

As with the physical clutter, the commitments we collect often start with good intentions:

- That volunteer role we took on to help out 'just for a few weeks'

- The weekly catch-up that stopped being joyful months ago

- The side hustle that started as a passion project and slowly turned into unpaid pressure.

What begins with a spark of joy can turn into a stack of tiring, joyless commitments. Before you know it, your calendar feels like an overstuffed closet — jammed, uneven and full of things you've outgrown but haven't let go of.

You have normalised exhaustion as if it's simply part of life, when in fact it's conditioning. And you've become used to running on empty.

Maybe it's time to embrace the principles of minimalism: the discipline of removing the excess so the meaningful has space to thrive.

It's like design thinking for life: fewer inputs, sharper outcomes.

This is why minimalism goes beyond clean spaces and tidy shelves. You choose a life that feels spacious, not just organised.

When you subtract the clutter, you get space, agency and breathing room to make decisions that align with who you are, not who you were trying to keep up with.

Think about it:

- A cupboard full of unworn clothes is just visual noise.

- A week full of obligations that no longer fit is existential noise.

We need to approach our time like our physical space, and edit our schedules the way we declutter our closets. By doing this, you are reclaiming discernment, because your calendar, like your home, should reflect who you are — not just what you've collected.

THE MINIMALIST MOVEMENT

You can trace the roots of minimalism back centuries, across cultures, philosophies and belief systems. The idea of a simpler life is ancient.

The Stoics of Ancient Greece practised minimalism as a form of discipline and peace. Zen monks in Japan turned it into art, embodying it through sparse gardens, calligraphy and silence. Spiritual leaders from the Buddha to Saint Francis of Assisi have spoken of the clarity that comes from owning less and needing less.

Modern minimalism, the kind we hear about in podcasts, see on Instagram feeds and read about in personal transformation blogs, emerged from a different kind of crisis: *too much.*

- Too much stuff

- Too many decisions

- Too many plates spinning — physically, mentally and emotionally.

Late in the first decade of the 2000s, as consumer culture peaked and digital overwhelm became the new normal, a quiet uprising began.

At first, it showed up as a lifestyle experiment. In Ohio, two corporate professionals, Joshua Fields Millburn and Ryan Nicodemus, began sharing their journey of letting go. First it was the extra clothes, then the unopened gadgets, then the pointless meetings and then, eventually, the expectations they'd built their entire careers around.

Their message was simple: don't live with nothing; live with *what matters*. They called themselves The Minimalists. What began as a blog became a bestselling book, a TEDx talk, a Netflix documentary and a movement that reached millions.

At the same time, across the Pacific, a softly spoken organising consultant from Tokyo was inviting people to hold their possessions and ask: 'Does this spark joy?' Marie Kondo's approach was ritualistic, almost spiritual — and her method was transformational. It gave people a way of saying thank you, letting go and making space for something more aligned. Her book sold over 10 million copies and changed how a generation thought about their relationship with stuff.

Then came the bloggers, the thinkers and the architects of slow. Writers like Leo Babauta and Courtney Carver championed simplicity as a lifestyle of intentional minimalism: less for the sake of focus, and space as a strategy.

What started in homes and inboxes began to move into boardrooms, classrooms and cities. What had once been a reaction to consumerism evolved into a redesign of life itself.

In Japan, people like Fumio Sasaki radically decluttered not just their apartments, but their sense of identity. Sasaki didn't just own fewer things; he felt more *himself.* His story became a bestseller in East Asia, sparking a wider conversation about self-worth, societal pressure and what it means to live deliberately in a crowded world.

In Brazil, a new generation of entrepreneurs began turning away from hyper-growth models, choosing localism, craftsmanship and sustainable pace over scale. The *vida simples* movement (meaning 'simple life') emerged as a counterbalance to hustle culture. Its message was clear: enough is not failure, it's freedom.

And in Sweden, an age-old tradition called *döstädning* ('Swedish death cleansing') took on new life. Rather than being morbid, it is a mindful, cultural practice of clearing out what you no longer need — not just to create order, but to leave behind peace. It is an act of care that outlives you.

A friend of mine lost her father last year. It was expected, but still heartbreaking. He'd lived a good, long life in the same home he and his wife had shared for more than 40 years.

When she arrived to start sorting through his things, she thought it might take a few days. A week, maybe.

It took months.

He hadn't touched much since her mother had died 15 years earlier. Her teacups were still in the same cupboard; her scarves were still folded in the drawer. Every card, every note, every travel brochure they'd ever collected was still tucked away in boxes, on bookshelves and in filing cabinets. It was nothing extreme, and they certainly weren't hoarders. They were just two people who had lived a full life and, like most of us, had kept things 'just in case' or because it felt too hard to decide what to let go of.

But now that decision belonged to their daughter.

What should be kept? What should be donated? What would be useful, meaningful or just too painful to throw away?

Every drawer opened a memory, and every cupboard reopened the grief.

She told me, 'I barely had space to grieve properly. I spent so much time making decisions about *things*, I didn't have time to feel what I was losing.'

There was no one to blame, and her parents hadn't done anything wrong. They were just doing what most of us do — accumulating as we move through life, deferring decisions and avoiding the discomfort of letting go while we're still here.

Minimalism isn't about sterile spaces or white walls (if it ever really was). It's not a restriction or a judgement but a return to what matters. Minimalism gives us the quiet courage to say:

- This is enough.
- This is me.
- This is what I choose to carry forward.

When you subtract what doesn't matter, what's left is *space* and that, more than any tactic or system, is what gives Red Brick Thinking its edge.

The minimalism movement began the moment someone, somewhere, stopped and said, 'I don't want to live like this anymore' and then they chose a different path. And then someone else did, and so a movement began.

This is intentional and strategic subtraction. What remains is aligned, energised and alive, and that same minimalist mindset ripples outward:

- In architecture, it influences the design of light, airy, adaptable buildings to create spaces that breathe.

- In tech, it's behind the rise of calm design and humane interfaces with tools that do what they promise and then get out of your way.

- In parenting, it reshapes the idea that children need full calendars to thrive. Instead, they need attention, conversation and time.

- In leadership, it creates workplaces that reward focus, not frantic energy, and that design for depth, not distraction.

- In life, it invites all of us to stop asking, 'How can I fit everything in?' and start asking, 'What's worth fitting in at all?'

CLUTTER ISN'T NEUTRAL

While there is the obvious financial cost of a purchase, there is also an ongoing, invisible cost. This cost can be felt in our energy, attention and emotions, and when we multiply that by thousands of items — across our homes, our digital lives and our to-do lists — the weight becomes crushing.

- **You feel it in the small jolt of frustration when you open a drawer and it's full of things you don't remember owning but can't quite throw away.** These things may include batteries that might still work, keys that probably don't fit anything and power cables you're sure belong to something … but what?

- **You notice it when something new enters your life (like a gift, a gadget or a document) and you feel a flash of irritation — not because of what it is, but because you don't know where it belongs.** There's no room, physically or mentally, so instead of delight, you feel the burden of one more thing.

- **You catch it in the moments of decision fatigue.** Such decisions are rarely big, life-changing choices, but more likely the constant sorting of cluttered categories. Perhaps you have five jackets, all almost the same; 30 unread emails, none of them urgent but all demanding a sliver of your attention; or calendar invites stacked like Tetris blocks. Every one of them feels vaguely important but they're deeply draining.

We carry too much, then wonder why we're tired all the time. This is the unspoken cost of accumulation. We think of 'stuff' as being static, but it takes up space, demands attention and holds memory and, over time, becomes a tax on your mind and a drain on your capacity.

And then there's the literal cost.

In Australia alone, over 67 million tonnes of waste is generated each year. A huge portion of that is discarded consumer goods, fast fashion, fast tech, fast everything. We buy on impulse and discard just as quickly. The average Australian household throws out 23 kilograms of clothing every year, much of it barely worn, and we repeat this cycle, season after season, because we've been sold the lie that more equals new, and new equals better.

Most people wear 20 per cent of their wardrobe 80 per cent of the time. We use a fraction of our kitchen gadgets, ignore unread books and store items 'just in case' that, deep down, we know we'll never touch again.

So why do we keep it? Because ownership is emotional, and we confuse attachment with usefulness. We mistake price tag for value ('But it was expensive ... '), and we let imagined futures stop us from living fully in the present.

Better doesn't come from volume; it comes from discernment about what matters.

The more we acquire, the harder it is to locate what actually matters because we lose time searching and we lose energy managing. Every unnecessary thing we carry — physically, mentally, organisationally — is pulling focus from something that deserves it more.

That's the paradox of accumulation. We think it adds to our lives, but often it buries us — and the cost isn't measured in dollars. It's measured in distraction.

Imagine what you could think about, create or feel if you weren't managing all this physical and mental clutter!

Red Brick Thinking requires discernment, and discernment creates space, and space — real, uncluttered space — isn't a luxury. It's a necessity.

YOUR RELATIONSHIP WITH STUFF

Let's get one thing clear: we're not just talking about objects. We're talking about what those objects represent — the meanings we assign to them and the emotions we've quietly tied up in them. Because your stuff (every drawer, every shelf, every forgotten box) tells a story, and often that story is louder than we realise.

- That jacket you haven't worn in years? It's not just fabric; it's the version of you who was going to go out more, be bolder, show up differently.

- The unopened box in the garage? It's not just storage; it's your deferred decisions, your emotional backlog and the things you've postponed dealing with.

- The piles of 'just in case' items? A drawerful of spare cables, duplicate utensils and unread books are not just a sign of being prepared. They're an indicator of control, anxiety and fear — of needing something and not having it.

Our belongings become a proxy for our identity, intentions and insecurities.

Over time, we carry them not because we love them, but because we don't know how to let them go. Decluttering is a way to clean up our lives, but it's also a way to wake ourselves up.

Decluttering invites us to stop living on autopilot and start asking real questions:

- Why did I bring this into my life in the first place?

- What story was I buying into?

- Does that story still reflect who I am today?

We don't just accumulate things; we accumulate assumptions, beliefs and aspirations that may have been useful once, but now sit quietly collecting dust.

Letting go of stuff is often the first visible act of something much deeper: reclaiming authorship over your life. When we let go:

- We say, 'I don't need to keep this just because I always have.'

- We recognise that space isn't something to fear but something to honour.

- We choose presence over the weight of old plans, past versions and unspoken guilt.

Letting go is especially powerful when you realise how little of what you own actually aligns with how you live.

So, open a drawer, stand in front of your bookshelf or walk through your hallway — not with a garbage bag, but with a question: 'What am I holding on to that no longer reflects who I am or who I want to become?'

When you start to let go — not all at once, but steadily, intentionally — something changes. Not just your space, but your sense of self. You begin to see what you actually need, what supports you and what reflects your current life — not the life you thought you'd be living five years ago.

And maybe, in the clearing, you'll remember who you are underneath all the things you thought you had to hold on to.

Chapter 8

Perfectionism

In the late 1990s, Jason Fried was a web designer freelancing out of Chicago, quietly observing the early chaos of the dot-com boom.

Launch big, dazzle investors, chase scale…this mindset was everywhere. Products were stuffed with features, teams were over-engineered, timelines ballooned and everything was built to make an impression as much as to deliver functionality.

But Fried saw something deeper driving it all: a quiet obsession with *perfection*, the belief that a product wasn't ready until it had everything. He saw a system where every idea, every option, every edge case had to be considered, and anything less than flawless remained unfinished.

He didn't buy it.

In 1999, Fried co-founded a small design firm called 37signals, grounded in a refreshingly bold (at the time) idea later championed by Sheryl Sandberg during her time at Facebook: *done is better than perfect.* Alongside co-owner David Heinemeier Hansson, Fried built 37signals' reputation not just on clean software, but on releasing real things, imperfectly, on purpose.

They didn't wait for every bell and whistle or obsess over polish. They shipped when the product was useful, not when it was finished. Sometimes it was messy, sometimes it was early, but it moved.

While others got stuck chasing a version of 'perfect' that never arrived, Fried and his team chose momentum.

From the beginning, Fried and his co-founders built their reputation not just on software, but on subtraction: design that didn't shout, interfaces that didn't overwhelm and products that shipped when they were ready, if not before.

When they launched Basecamp in 2004, it was intentionally minimal. No bloat, no bells and no whistles. It did one thing: helped teams manage projects without drowning in email. The interface was simple, the code was clean and the features were few. It looked, by some Silicon Valley standards, almost unfinished.

And that was the point.

Fried believed that perfectionism was a trap: that the obsession with launching things 'just right' delayed real value, real feedback and real connection. To him, perfection was where good ideas went to die, buried under delay, scope creep and self-doubt.

Fried valued other qualities:

- Instead of chasing refinement, he chased momentum.

- Instead of building for scale, he built for usefulness.

- Instead of treating simplicity as a compromise, he treated it as a feature.

And it worked.

Quietly growing through word of mouth, Basecamp became one of the most used project management tools in the world, and an alternative blueprint for building a business.

Fried didn't stop there. He and Hansson went on to write *Getting Real, Rework, Remote* and *It Doesn't Have to Be Crazy at Work*, books that read like manifestos for Red Brick Thinking in tech. Each one challenged a cultural obsession with always-on hustle, perfectionism and scale for scale's sake. They argued for transparency over control, action over aesthetics, small teams over sprawling org charts, and launching early over waiting forever.

One of their core practices was intentionally shipping 'unfinished' features. These features weren't broken and the business wasn't being lazy; the features were ready enough to be useful, so the next step was to learn from the launch.

In one of their books, Fried writes, 'You can endlessly tweak something, but you'll never know if it's any good until you get it in front of real people.'

In other words:

- Launch, then listen.

- Make it useful, not perfect.

- Build something simple and let it grow from there.

In an industry that still idolises the perfect pitch deck, the flawless product demo and the shiny corporate veneer, Fried remains an outlier. He never wanted to be impressive; he wanted to be honest, and that meant walking away from perfectionism early and never looking back.

Sometimes the most powerful thing you can do is to release bravely rather than refine endlessly.

Red Brick Thinking calls for subtraction of the need to prove, perfect and protect.

JUST ONE MORE TWEAK

Perfectionism often dresses up as quality control. It wears the language of standards and excellence, but most of the time it's just fear in a tailored suit. This fear can arise in many forms: fear of being judged, fear of not being good enough or fear of releasing something that feels incomplete — because it means *you* might feel incomplete too.

And so, we tweak, hover, rewrite the email, re-edit the file and reread the draft for the twelfth time. We do this not because we need to, but because we're afraid to let go.

In creative work, this paralysis is especially dangerous. Whole projects die inside version 19.3, held hostage by the myth that perfect is just one more pass away.

Perfectionism also shows up in leadership, in parenting, in performance reviews. It's the extra slide in the deck, the over-explained email or the reluctance to delegate because no one else will do it 'right'.

Perfectionism slows everything down — and what's worse, it shrinks us. It keeps our best ideas in drafts, and our boldest moves in delay. It convinces us that if we just keep refining, we'll be safe.

This is the Red Brick of Perfection: the belief that if something isn't flawless, it isn't worthy.

PERFECT ISN'T A STANDARD; IT'S A STORY

Perfectionism is deeply rooted in how we're wired to seek control, safety and approval.

Paul Hewitt and Gordon Flett, two of the leading psychologists in this field, tell us that perfectionism tends to fall into three categories:

- *Self-oriented perfectionism,* where we impose impossibly high standards on ourselves
- *Socially prescribed perfectionism,* where we believe others expect us to be perfect
- *Other-oriented perfectionism,* where we project those standards onto the people around us.

Hewitt and Flett claim that the most toxic version is socially prescribed perfectionism. It's the version most linked to anxiety, burnout, depression and even imposter syndrome, because we're not just trying to be good, we're trying to be *good enough for everyone else* — and that's a moving target. This has no doubt led to perfectionism among young people dramatically increasing over the past three decades. Social media, academic pressure and workplace competitiveness have all created a climate where 'not good enough' and comparison has become normal.

Perfection taps directly into the brain's reward circuitry. Each time we fix, tweak or polish, we get a small dopamine hit — not just for achieving something, but for the anticipation of improvement. It feels productive, even virtuous, reinforcing a cycle of striving that's more about the rush of 'almost there' than actual progress.

The research also found that perfectionists often hold a deep belief that their worth is conditional on performance, presentation or approval. So, the stakes feel higher than just getting it right. It feels personal.

PERFECT, BUT AT WHAT PRICE?

The Red Brick of Perfectionism becomes armour. It's a defence mechanism dressed up as thoroughness:

- We fine-tune every email.
- We say yes to things we don't have the capacity for.
- We can't hit 'send' until it's just right, because we're afraid of what people will think if it's not flawless.

This is beyond ego. We fear being seen as difficult, incompetent or selfish, or we fear letting someone down — even if the person we're disappointing is ourselves.

In psychology, this shows up as fawning: a trauma response, where we appease others to maintain safety. In the workplace, it gets rewarded, praised and promoted.

- We don't call it people pleasing — we call it 'a strong work ethic'.

- We don't name the anxiety — we call it 'professionalism'.

- We don't recognise the burnout — we just pour another coffee and push through.

This is where perfectionism thrives: not in laziness, but in over-functioning and trying to be all things to all people, without ever asking, 'What would happen if I didn't?'

'HIGH STANDARDS' MEANS LOW TRUST

Perfectionism loves to hide behind praise: 'You just have such high standards.' 'You're detail oriented.' 'You always go above and beyond.' It shows up as excellence, discipline and pride in the work.

- **You notice a subtle resistance to letting anyone else take the reins.** Even when you delegate, you double-check, you rewrite and you hover. You know they're capable, but you don't quite trust that it will be done *right* — and 'right' often just means *your way.*

- **You feel uneasy when things unfold without your direct involvement.** You say you're flexible, that you trust the process, but a part of you still wants to steer from the backseat. When you're not holding the plan tightly, it feels like it might slip through your fingers.

- **You find that your so-called 'high standards' have less to do with excellence and more to do with control.** Underneath it all is a quiet fear that if you don't stay on top of everything, something or someone will fall apart.

- **You realise that what you're really protecting isn't the work; it's yourself.** That perfect, glossy version of yourself is a kind of shield. The idea of being seen in progress, in process or in any form less than perfect feels like a risk you'd rather not take.

Red Brick Thinking asks us to look more closely. Are you focused on the work, or are you protecting your identity as 'the reliable one'?

You see this not just in boardrooms or studios, but in classrooms, kitchens and community halls. And the costs of perfection can be seen in all parts of our lives:

- **In relationships.** Hiding the mess means hiding your real self.

- **In work.** The best ideas die through over-editing.

- **In life.** The good gets buried under the chase for great.

THE RELIABLE ONE

Some perfectionism starts in ambition, but a lot of it starts in approval.

From a young age, many of us learn that being useful equals being loved, that being helpful equals being safe, and that the fastest way to avoid disappointment is to keep everyone around you happy.

So, we become good at it. No, *really* good at it:

- We anticipate needs before they're spoken.

- We show up early.

- We over-prepare.

- We double-check everything.

We do this not just to meet expectations, but to make sure no one ever has to feel let down by us.

At some point, that becomes who we are: the reliable one, the safe pair of hands, the person who never drops the ball, even when we're barely keeping it together.

When my friend Ava was seven, her mum started calling her 'my little helper'. It was meant with love. She'd fetch nappies for her baby brother, set the table without being asked and translate adult conversations into simpler words when things got tense. She was quick, capable and quiet.

By the time she was a teenager, no one ever worried about Ava. She got good grades, made her own lunches and didn't cause trouble. She knew how to read a room and smooth things over before emotions overspilled. She was, as everyone said, 'so mature for her age'.

What they didn't see was how hard she was working to earn that title.

Fast-forward 20 years, and Ava had a full life, career, family and home, but underneath it all was the same quiet pressure: to be the steady one, be across everything, anticipate needs before they're voiced, not drop the ball and not ask for too much.

She never thought of herself as a perfectionist. She thought of herself as *responsible*. She wasn't looking for gold stars and rewards. All she wanted was to keep everyone else afloat. The cost was subtle, rather than obvious: she never felt fully relaxed, and she was never quite sure when it was okay to let go.

It wasn't until I asked her, over coffee one day, 'When do you get to be the messy one?' that something shifted.

She didn't have an answer. Being the reliable one had become so fused with her identity, she didn't know who she was without it.

That was the beginning of the subtraction: letting someone else handle dinner; admitting she needed a break and leaving a message unread without guilt; small, deliberate rebellions against the idea that her value was in holding it all together.

Ava's not trying to be perfect anymore. She's just present, and that's what makes her truly reliable … not the doing, but the *being*.

Red Brick Thinking invites you to stop polishing your presence and start protecting your peace. It encourages you to ask, 'Is this actually mine to carry?' rather than 'Will they like me?' It helps you realise that being reliable doesn't mean being available to everyone at all times.

People-pleasing is not kindness; it's self-abandonment in slow motion. Perfectionism is often just people-pleasing with a spreadsheet.

But remember:

- You don't need to be everything to be enough.

- You don't need to be impressive to be valued.

- You don't need to earn love by erasing your limits.

The version of you that's good enough already exists.

Perfectionism is a heavy anchor. When you finally drop it, you release the need to impress, to please and to prove that what's left is not a mess — it's momentum.

You don't have to be perfect; you just have to get moving.

PERFECTIONISM AS A DELAY TACTIC

We rarely call perfectionism what it is — we just say we're 'not ready yet'. We call it fine-tuning, quality assurance or strategy, but often what we're really doing is delaying, hiding and avoiding the release of the work due to the risk of it being seen before it's perfect. As a result:

- The message stays in draft.

- The website stays in staging.

- The book never gets published.

- The project never gets launched.

We feel it's safer to keep editing than to put something imperfect into the world.

Progress dies from waiting for perfect.

In 2019, a small Melbourne-based studio released something weird, unpolished and simple.

The team at House House had never expected to go viral. They were four friends making a game about a mischievous goose terrorising a quaint British village. That's it. No weapons, no scoring and no complicated mechanics. Just honking, stealing and chaos.

They could've overbuilt it, smoothed the rough edges, added levels, added lore, added drama ... but they didn't.

Instead, they let it be simple — and in doing so, they let it be fun.

Untitled Goose Game became a global phenomenon. It topped download charts and won multiple international awards. It was played by celebrities and streamed by millions, and all without the kind of obsessive, perfectionist development cycle that plagues so much of the creative world.

In interviews, the developers admitted they weren't chasing perfection. They were chasing delight, and they trusted that the charm of the game didn't lie in adding more, but in knowing when to stop.

> *That's the red brick move: not to rush and not to cut corners, but to release the idea before perfectionism strangles its momentum.*

Perfection comes from letting the work go.

So, if you find yourself stuck in one more edit, one more draft, one more meeting before your project is 'ready', ask yourself: 'Am I improving this? Or just protecting myself from what happens next?'

The trap of perfectionism is that it masquerades as professionalism when, really, it's a form of procrastination.

Red Brick Thinking doesn't lower the bar; it shifts the goal:

- From flawless to real

- From safe to useful

- From hidden to visible.

Waiting for perfect is just a slower way to fail. *Letting go of perfect* is how you finally begin to make things happen.

PART 3
STRUCTURAL RED BRICKS

Some red bricks are architectural. They live in the design of our days, our systems and our spaces, and they quietly hold us back.

Structural Red Bricks create friction we can feel but don't always see, such as a clunky workflow, a bloated process or a tech stack that creates more work than it saves. These are the hidden obstacles that drain momentum and make everything harder than it needs to be.

We tend to blame ourselves when things stall, assuming we need more motivation or willpower. But often the issue isn't personal — it's structural. When we shift the structure, action becomes easier.

In this part of the book, you'll meet five of the most common structural culprits:

- Friction
- Complexity
- Noise
- Stimulation
- Urgency.

Each one can grind at your day — but when we strip them back, progress speeds up.

Chapter 9

Friction

n 2006 Melanie Perkins was a university student teaching graphic design software to her peers. She kept noticing the same frustration playing out again and again: they had ideas and they had vision, but the tools got in the way. Hours were lost navigating clunky menus, mastering steep learning curves and wrestling with interfaces that made even simple tasks feel out of reach. They weren't struggling with their imagination; they were struggling with friction.

The software they were using was technically powerful: Adobe Photoshop, InDesign, Illustrator. Industry standard products with decades of development; however, to access that power, you had to fight your way through it. Endless toolbars buried menus and unfamiliar icons. Just opening each program felt like stepping into a cockpit.

The design work itself came easily, but the hard part was getting to the point where you could even begin.

The default response in tech had always been the same — add more features, power and options — but Perkins saw something different. What if the real opportunity lay in removing the barriers between idea and execution, rather than adding more tools?

That insight became Canva: a platform designed to accelerate human momentum rather than slow people down with complicated software. Drag, drop, done. No steep learning curve and no design degree required. What once took hours could now take minutes — not because people got smarter, but because the friction had been cleared.

The industry laughed, questioning if this was 'real design', but Perkins wasn't building for professionals who'd already invested in mastering the mess. She was building a product for the billions of people who just wanted to bring ideas to life without getting stuck at step one.

By removing friction and resistance, Canva unlocked creativity and opened the floodgates.

Canva didn't win by doing more. It won by clearing the path.

THE DRAG YOU LEARN TO LIVE WITH

The Red Brick of Friction lives everywhere: in our systems, our processes, our meetings, our assumptions. We often don't see it, but we can feel it in the effort required to do what should be simple.

This friction is not the obvious, dramatic kind that stops you in your tracks, but the subtle, silent effort that wears you down over time. It slows you down like sand in the gears, making simple things feel hard. It tells people, 'This isn't for you.'

Friction is the unnecessary resistance baked into the way we work, lead, plan and communicate:

- The convoluted process that no one questions

- The clunky software interface

- The weekly meeting that goes nowhere

- The approval system that turns momentum into molasses.

It hides inside 'how we've always done things' and dresses itself as due diligence, policy, tradition and even professionalism — but underneath, it's pure drag.

The tricky part is that we rarely name it as a problem. We get used to it, build workarounds and train ourselves to tolerate it... we even reward it, such as when we thank the team for pulling an all-nighter without asking why it was necessary. Friction becomes the cost of doing business, of doing life, until one day we realise we're spending more time navigating the system than delivering value inside it.

Friction shows up when:

- A new hire can't figure out how to request leave

- A customer drops out because the sign-up form is too confusing

- A brilliant idea dies in the third round of approvals.

It doesn't arise because people aren't smart or capable, but because the path is cluttered.

Friction is easy to miss because there aren't any childish tantrums; it just slowly kills energy and reduces momentum.

Friction is a signal, and it's time to start listening.

WHEN EFFORT FEELS LIKE PROOF

Friction is sneaky. We don't just tolerate it; we justify it. Somewhere along the way, we've absorbed the idea that if something's a struggle, it must be worthwhile, and that a little resistance is the price of doing important work.

We rarely question whether the resistance is necessary — we just assume it belongs. This is called the *mere exposure effect*: the more we're exposed to something, the more we tend to accept or like it, even if it's inefficient. In organisations, repeated exposure to poor processes breeds familiarity, which we mistake for functionality.

We are almost wired to *respect* friction. In a study published in 1959, psychologists Elliot Aronson and Judson Mills found that participants who underwent more difficult or embarrassing initiations to join a group rated the group more positively, even when the content was dull. The harder it is, the more we feel it must matter.

Likewise, when we put a lot of effort into something, we tend to overvalue the result, regardless of whether the effort was necessary. It's a form of cognitive dissonance reduction: if this was hard, it must be worth it.

In organisations, friction becomes tradition:

- Layers of approval are seen as safeguards.

- Long meetings signal commitment.

- Complex systems are mistaken for sophistication.

Every added step becomes a legacy of someone's good intention, left in place long after the original problem has disappeared. We also tend to prefer things to stay as they are, especially when change introduces uncertainty — even if the current system is inefficient.

Status quo bias describes the idea that people consistently favour existing processes, even when better options are available, simply because they feel more 'known'. And then there's the pride we feel when we make it work: 'It's complicated, but I've figured it out.' This leads us to become gatekeepers of clunky tools and tangled workflows, mistaking mastery of complexity for value, instead of asking why the system is so hard to begin with.

Friction feels fair. If we had to struggle through something, shouldn't everyone else? This unconscious belief keeps inefficient processes alive, especially in hierarchies: 'We earned it the hard way, and so should you!'

At a personal level, friction gives us a false sense of progress. But we are confusing activity with effectiveness. And spinning your wheels without moving is burnout in disguise.

We hold on to friction because we've stopped noticing it and made peace with inefficiency. We don't want to rock the boat.

DEATH BY A THOUSAND CLICKS

Friction wears you down.

Friction is not the kind of resistance that stops progress outright; it's the kind that makes everything feel just a bit harder, slower and heavier. Over time, that adds up to real fatigue, lost time, wasted energy and missed opportunities.

- In teams, friction erodes momentum. It turns collaboration into confusion and slows projects down — not because the ideas are flawed, but because no one can find the right version of the file or figure out who needs to approve what. People stop suggesting improvements because even small changes feel like a battle.

- In leadership, friction shows up as sluggish decision-making, bloated strategies and the sense that you're always reacting but never really moving forward. The path is cluttered, so progress feels like pushing a wheelbarrow through mud — doable, but exhausting.

- For individuals, the cost is subtle but corrosive. You start avoiding certain tasks because the steps involved are clunky or unclear. You waste cognitive energy just navigating systems and you lose enthusiasm due to inefficiency.

Friction silently chips away at your capacity to care.

When things take too long or feel too hard, we often don't blame the system — we blame ourselves. We think we're inefficient, lazy or unmotivated, but we're not the problem: the friction is.

Friction has a hidden price tag, and most teams, leaders and organisations are paying for it in missed momentum.

WHEN SIMPLE THINGS FEEL HARD

You feel friction long before you see it.

- **You realise how bloated things have become when you have to Google how to do something inside your own organisation.** When the process becomes too convoluted, even the people who built it can't explain it clearly.

- **You feel it when a simple task, like booking leave, submitting expenses or onboarding a new client, starts to feel like threading a needle blindfolded.** Too many steps, too many approvals and no one's quite sure why it works that way — but no one's changed it, either.

- **You hear it in how people talk about tools.** 'It's a bit clunky.' 'I just avoid that system.' 'Oh, don't use that, it's a nightmare.' Entire platforms go unused because they weren't designed with humans in mind.

- **You catch yourself saying, 'I'll just do it manually.'** You're not being stubborn; you've just recognised that the workaround is easier than the official process. You're not resisting structure; you're dodging inefficiency.

- **You notice how tiny tasks feel strangely heavy.** The task isn't difficult, but the *process* is — and somewhere between opening the tab and finding the right login, your energy disappears.

- **You watch collaboration stall.** No one's sure where the doc lives, who owns what or what happens next. So, they wait — and while they wait, momentum dies.

On a more personal level, friction sounds like:

- 'Why does this take so long?'

- 'I know there's a better way to do this, but I don't have the time to figure it out.'

- 'This shouldn't be this hard.'

The worst part is that friction makes you question yourself: you wonder if you're missing something, if everyone else is somehow managing, if the problem is you instead of the broken system you're operating within.

Friction gaslights you.

Red Brick Thinking teaches us to pause and look again. When work feels harder than it should, it's rarely because people aren't working hard — it tends to be caused by the friction that no one's dared to question.

In 2010, brothers Patrick and John Collison asked a deceptively simple question: 'Why is it so hard to accept payments online?'

At the time, setting up online payments was a maze of bank relationships, merchant accounts, compliance paperwork and clunky code. For startups and developers, it was a slow, painful process and a source of friction that killed momentum before businesses even launched.

Most people in the payments world accepted it as 'just how it works'. It was complex because money is complex, but the Collisons saw the friction for what it really was: outdated systems, legacy rules and needless complexity layered over time.

So, they didn't add more features — they removed the friction.

Stripe was built around a simple idea: accepting payments should be as easy as dropping a few lines of code into your website. No faxes, phone calls or weeks of waiting — just a clean, developer-first interface and a smooth onboarding flow that took minutes, not months.

Stripe didn't just power a few websites: it quietly became the financial infrastructure behind companies like Shopify, Amazon, Atlassian and Airbnb. At the time of writing, it's valued at over US$130 billion. Its success came not because it added complexity to an already crowded space, but because it removed the unnecessary effort that was blocking innovation. Stripe saw the invisible resistance and cleared it.

Just like Canva did for design, Stripe disrupted finance by removing the intimidation layer from commerce.

When you remove friction, you don't just make things easier. You make them possible.

CLEARING THE PATH, NOT REBUILDING THE ROAD

You don't need to burn everything down to remove friction; you need to notice where effort is being wasted and have the courage to simplify.

Friction thrives in places we've stopped questioning, such as legacy processes, clunky tech and policies built for problems that no longer exist. The first step is to see the lag for what it is: not a necessary evil, but a solvable problem.

Friction lives in the workarounds:

- It's the spreadsheet someone created because the system doesn't do what it should.
- It's the Slack channel that replaces the bloated team meeting.

Every workaround is a red flag waving quietly in the distance.

Letting go starts with subtraction, not overhaul: remove a step, cancel a meeting, kill a form no one needs, eliminate the fourth round of approval.

In other words, you need to remove the resistance that makes the work harder than it needs to be.

If you're a leader, make it safe to name the friction, not just push through it. Too often, people assume nothing can change until someone says it can — and people don't always want to put their hand up and raise a problem that needs solving.

When you start subtracting with purpose, something powerful happens: space opens up, energy returns and flow reappears.

You don't always need better tools, more time or a new system. Sometimes you just need to clear what's in the way.

SLOW IS SMOOTH AND SMOOTH IS FAST

We've been conditioned to believe that struggle builds character, that hard equals important and that if something feels easy, it's probably not serious enough.

Friction makes things clunkier, and more exhausting.

My niece Alex served in the military. During her training, she was taught how to break down, clean and reassemble her weapon, over and over again, until it was second nature.

At first, she rushed. Everyone did. There was pressure to prove how capable you were by how quickly you could finish. Speed looked like skill and fast meant ready.

But their instructors kept pulling them back.

'Slow is smooth,' they'd say. 'And smooth is fast.'

It didn't make sense at first. It sounded like one of those sayings you nod at without really understanding.

But over time, she got it.

When she tried to move too fast, she fumbled. Pieces dropped, steps got missed and, in the rush to finish, she ended up slower.

But when she slowed down, everything changed. Her breathing steadied, her hands moved with purpose, the motions became cleaner and more deliberate and, without trying, her speed improved—not because she was pushing, but because she was flowing.

That phrase stuck with her long after her training.

And when she shared it with me, it stuck with me too.

Because most of us are rushing through tasks, through decisions and through life. We mistake movement for momentum, and urgency for importance, but real efficiency isn't frantic — it's fluid.

'Slow is smooth and smooth is fast' isn't just about weapons training: it's about how we work, how we lead and how we live. Subtraction starts when we realise that doing fewer things with greater intention will always beat doing more things in a blur.

The smartest teams, leaders and systems aren't the ones doing the most; they're the ones doing the least in their own way. They've cleared the path so energy flows where it matters.

The smoothest path is the one you finally cleared.

Friction is a signal to simplify.

Remove the drag and reclaim the flow, because progress shouldn't feel like a battle every time.

Chapter 10

Complexity

When you think of the most powerful forces in global entertainment, a six-year-old blue heeler from Brisbane probably doesn't top the list.

And yet *Bluey* has become one of the most beloved children's shows in the world. It's the most-streamed program on ABC iview and the most downloaded on BBC iPlayer, and its gentle, funny stories reach over 60 countries. One recent season drew more than 11 million viewers.

Here's the surprising part: it's a show where not much happens. At least, not at first glance. It doesn't have villains, superpowers or flashy animation. It's just a dog family — Mum, Dad and two kids — navigating the small stuff: bedtime, backyard games and learning to wait.

Bluey is a masterclass in simplicity.

Where most creators chase more features or polish, *Bluey* subtracts. Its seven-minute episodes contain strong storytelling, emotional truth and space to breathe. It resonates not because it shouts, but because it listens.

Bluey didn't win the world over by being the flashiest; it won by being the simplest.

In a 2024 interview with entertainment news site Deadline, *Bluey* creator Joe Brumm shared his thoughts on why *Bluey* is so popular with both kids and adults. 'The episodes that have cut through with adults are based on something real,' said Brumm. 'Usually, they're related to something I've learned having kids … An episode really wouldn't start until I'd found a bit of truth like that. I wouldn't necessarily understand it and often the episode is an exploration of that.'

That's Red Brick Thinking. Strip it back, keep what matters, and say no — so you can say yes to quality.

THE CULT OF COMPLEXITY

We rarely choose complexity on purpose. It sneaks in, masquerading as rigour, sophistication and sometimes even strategy:

- We add policies to cover every possibility.
- We create tools to manage tools.
- We build workflows that require a user manual, then add training to explain the manual.

We don't do this because we're careless, but because we've absorbed the idea that important things should be hard.

In many organisations, complexity isn't just tolerated — it's rewarded. The person with the longest presentation, the most detailed dashboard or the cleverest acronyms looks like the expert, even if no one understands a word they're saying.

Research shows that we tend to equate complexity with intelligence, depth or seriousness. In fact, studies by psychologist Daniel Oppenheimer found that people often perceive overly complex language or systems as more intelligent, even when they're less effective. This is called the complexity bias.

We assume that if something's intricate or hard to explain, it must be sophisticated. It's why we overstuff our slide decks, overexplain in meetings or create bloated workflows. Complexity gives the illusion of value, even when it's just filler.

And because complexity takes effort to unpack, we stop questioning it. We nod along, we adapt and we fill in the gaps ourselves until the entire system is being held together by workarounds and unspoken assumptions.

Simplicity can look too easy and too exposed. When we remove layers of process, polish or padding, it can feel like we're doing less, not more. According to psychologists Amos Tversky and Daniel Kahneman and their work on loss aversion, people are more sensitive to what they lose than what they gain. So when we remove something, even if it's unnecessary, it can feel like a loss.

Complexity feeds off our silence, growing in the cracks between intention and action, between what's said and what's done — and the longer it goes unchecked, the more permanent it feels.

When we embrace complexity, we are often hiding behind jargon, legacy and the fear that if we make something simple, it might look too easy, too obvious or too … unimportant.

Adding rules, policies, layers or tools gives us a false sense of control. It's a protection mechanism: *if we just add another layer, we'll avoid risk.* But as systems thinker Donella Meadows argued, beyond a certain point, every new layer reduces flexibility and responsiveness — the very things we need most in complexity.

Red Brick Thinking doesn't fall for it.

It rarely sees complexity as a sign of brilliance; more often, it sees complexity as a sign of drift away from purpose and momentum.

When complexity looks like competence, we confuse convoluted with clever.

THE UNSUSTAINABLE COSTS

The cost of complexity is erosion:

- It erodes comprehension by making everything take longer to explain.

- It erodes momentum by requiring six steps for something that should take one.

- It erodes trust when no one's quite sure who's accountable, or how things really work.

In organisations, complexity creates the illusion of sophistication, while quietly killing speed and adaptability:

- People stop asking questions because they're afraid of sounding uninformed.

- Teams spend more time managing the process than doing the work.

- Leaders assume they're being strategic but can't explain the strategy without a slide deck and a glossary.

In systems, complexity multiplies. Every new tool brings another integration, every new rule brings another exception, and every 'just in case' becomes another roadblock for the people trying to move forward.

And then there's the human cost — the exhaustion that comes from working inside a system that feels more like a maze than a map. Decision fatigue sets in, meetings multiply and talented people start to disengage — not because they don't care, but because everything feels heavier than it needs to be.

We don't always recognise it as complexity. Sometimes, we just feel stuck.

Red Brick Thinking calls complexity what it is: unnecessary, unsustainable and deeply expensive in terms of time, attention, energy and trust.

The real risk of complexity isn't that things take longer — it's that we forget what we were trying to do in the first place.

LOOKS ORGANISED, FEELS CONFUSING

Complexity rarely shows up as chaos. More often, it hides in the everyday, dressed as meticulousness and masked as maturity. But there are quiet and repetitive signs that a system isn't streamlined, it's swollen.

- **You notice it when you're invited to a meeting … to prepare for another meeting.** Time is wasted planning how to plan at a pre-meeting before the meeting, with layers of discussion but no decisions made.

- **You see it when a project kicks off and no one's quite sure who's doing what.** Roles are fuzzy, accountability is assumed, and three people start building the same slide deck because no one was really clear about task ownership.

- **You feel it when your strategy takes more than one sentence to explain or, worse, more than one slide.** If it needs a keynote to make sense, it's probably not that clear.

- **You remember the fanfare of a new software rollout, followed by the quiet fade out.** Videos, town hall meetings, a launch deck with its own launch deck arrive with a bang, but no one's using it six months later because no one knows *how* to use it.

- **You hear it in hallway whispers about approvals.** No clear processes, just insider knowledge: 'You've got to run it past her first, then check if he's in a good mood, then maybe you'll get it through.'

- **You realise your tech stack has turned on itself.** You have a tool to manage your tools, and yet no one knows where the real document lives. People default to email — not because it's the best, but because it's the least broken.

- **You keep adding checks and steps to prevent mistakes, only to find the mistakes still happen — there's just more admin attached.** Complexity is pretending to be safety, while focus gets buried under process.

- **You see it in the way people quietly abandon the official process.** The steps are there, the policy's written … but no one follows it. They're not rebelling against the system, but the path is so clunky that they've had to build faster workarounds just to get things done.

These aren't productivity problems — they're friction signals. When these signals pile up, creativity slows, decision-making gets stuck, trust thins, and people stop taking initiative because they're stuck navigating systems that take more than they give.

Recognising complexity is the first move; removing it is the real work.

STAY LEAN TO KEEP MOVING

At its peak, the Roman Empire was an unrivalled superpower, stretching across Europe, North Africa and the Middle East. Its military strength, engineering marvels and bureaucratic efficiency made it one of the most formidable civilisations in history. Yet by the fifth century, it had crumbled. While historians debate the precise reasons for Rome's collapse, one underlying cause is strikingly relevant today: complexity overload.

Rome became a victim of its own success. As it expanded, so did its administrative burden, military costs and bureaucratic layers. What was once a lean and effective governance model transformed into an unwieldy, sluggish machine. With more provinces to manage, more laws to enforce and more enemies to defend against, Rome found itself drowning in its own excesses.

Emperor after emperor introduced new taxes, regulations and military campaigns, each adding layers of complication rather than stripping away inefficiencies. By the time Rome fell, its currency had been debased, its economy was unsustainable and its people had lost their faith in Rome's leadership. The empire collapsed not in a single, dramatic moment, but under the slow and steady weight of unchecked complexity.

Interestingly, while Rome was weighed down by excess, the so-called barbarian tribes — the Picts, Teutons and Vandals — thrived due to their simplicity. Unlike the Romans, who relied on vast supply chains, complex logistics and bureaucratic hierarchies, these more primitive societies operated with leaner structures. They had fewer administrative burdens, more flexible governance and a lifestyle that was naturally adapted to hardship.

In 2004, my sister and I observed this kind of difference when we travelled to Vietnam and, like many visitors, took a tour of the Cu Chi tunnels just outside of Ho Chi Minh City. At first, we treated it like a typical tourist excursion — something to tick off the list — but once we arrived, respect took over. The tunnels were astonishingly narrow; despite not being overly large people, we had to crouch and shuffle uncomfortably just to fit. They had in fact expanded many of the sections to allow tourists to move through them.

These tunnels were beyond engineering — they were a marvel in strategy. During the Vietnam War, the Viet Cong used them to evade heavily armed and well-equipped United States troops. While American soldiers carried packs full of gear, weapons and tools, the Viet Cong slipped underground in thin clothing, disappearing into a network invisible to the eye and impenetrable to heavy boots.

What looked like an advantage — more gear, more power, more protection — became a burden. The American troops were outfitted for dominance, but the Viet Cong were built for adaptability. Complexity slowed one side down, while simplicity made the other unstoppable.

When organisations, societies or individuals pile on obligations, rules and complexity without questioning their necessity, they become rigid and fragile, unable to adapt when it matters most. Just as Rome collapsed under the weight of its own systems, and United States forces were outmanoeuvred by Viet Cong fighters moving lightly through the tunnels, the lesson is clear: success belongs to those who keep it simple enough to move.

MAKE IT MAKE SENSE

It takes more discipline to say one thing clearly than ten things vaguely, and it takes more confidence to choose a single direction than to hedge with multiple layers. Simplicity demands understanding, whereas complexity requires vocabulary.

While many corporate mission statements read like committee-approved puzzles ('...to leverage synergies across core competencies to maximise stakeholder value' — cue eyeroll), Patagonia opted for something different: 'We're in business to save our home planet.'

Eight words. No buzzwords, embellishment or confusion, just conviction.

In its early years, Patagonia, like many values-driven companies, struggled with the balance between activism and commerce. As it grew, so did the pressure to formalise: to adopt the corporate norms of strategy statements, layered goals and the language of business-speak.

But founder Yvon Chouinard resisted. A lifelong climber and environmentalist, he believed that if you couldn't explain what you stood for clearly, you probably didn't stand for it at all.

The clarity of its mission gave Patagonia focus:

- It made decision-making easier.
- It allowed the company to turn down lucrative partnerships that clashed with its values.
- It took bold environmental stances. For example, it gave 1 per cent of sales to grassroots environmental groups, even before that became fashionable.

And in 2022, Chouinard went a step further, relinquishing ownership entirely and placing the company's profits into a trust designed to fight climate change.

That's what simplicity unlocks: not just clearer messaging, but clearer action.

Compare that to the organisations where the strategy lives in a 74-slide deck, updated quarterly but rarely read; where teams sit through planning meetings filled with frameworks so abstract they feel like satire; and where no one can quite explain what the company is really trying to do, just that they're 'moving the needle on key priorities in a competitive landscape'. Yawn.

Red Brick Thinking invites a different approach.

> *Ask your team: 'If this disappeared, who would miss it?' If the answer is 'no one', you've identified your red brick.*

When it comes to strategy, challenge the impulse to add. Before you launch another pillar, another program or another performance framework, ask what it will replace, because complexity grows by default and simplicity requires intention.

Red Brick Thinking asks: what if the smartest person in the room isn't the one who speaks in the most complex sentences, but the one who makes things make sense? Because complexity might impress in the short term, but sense-making scales, leads and moves.

And sometimes, the boldest thing you can do in a boardroom full of frameworks is to say something simple and mean it.

CLEAR BEATS CLEVER

We've been taught that complexity means sophistication — that the more layers something has, the more valuable it must be — but the cost of complexity is quiet and constant. It slows you down, clouds decisions, drains energy and turns everyday tasks into endurance tests.

You don't have to overhaul everything — just subtract one piece of unnecessary effort, and then another.

Simplicity isn't about cutting corners; it's about cutting through.

Chapter 11

Noise

I n 2009, Netflix released a culture deck that broke the internet, at least in corporate terms. It didn't look like much — no branding, no design, just black text on white slides — but what it said cut through the noise of corporate jargon like a scalpel:

- 'Adequate performance gets a generous severance package.'

- 'We're a team, not a family.'

- 'We try to get rid of rules when we can.'

Netflix didn't just talk about culture; it subtracted everything that got in the way of it. Instead of values carved in stone and ignored in practice, the deck became a blueprint for real-time decisions — no fluff and theatre, just clarity. And it spread because it was rare: simple, sharp and startlingly honest.

While most companies were adding values, pillars, principles and codes of conduct, Netflix removed what didn't help.

That's the power of subtracting noise.

THE VOLUME THAT DROWNS THE SIGNAL

We tend to think of noise as a technical problem, like static in a transmission.

But in work and in life, noise is rarely that obvious. It doesn't announce itself with sparks or sirens; it creeps in slowly, until what once felt sharp now feels sluggish, and what once moved cleanly now grinds with resistance.

The Red Brick of Noise is anything that distorts understanding, dulls momentum or blocks meaning. It's the invisible tax we pay on progress. It eats away at time, trust and attention — not in loud, dramatic ways, but in quiet, incremental ones.

It doesn't always look broken. In fact, it often looks like it's working:

- A detailed report delivered on time ... that no one reads

- A well-attended meeting ... that doesn't move anything forward

- A dashboard packed with metrics ... that obscure what matters most.

These are all forms of noise: complexity, excess and distraction dressed up as commitment.

Noise hides in the systems, tools, workflows, meetings and habits we've built. But they're not inherently flawed; they were built for a context that may no longer exist, and when the context changes but the structure stays the same, noise is what fills the gap.

It shows up as:

- **Interference.** Inputs that demand attention but add no value, such as notifications, updates, alerts, status checks, unread tabs and Slack threads that spiral into nowhere.

- **Waste.** Layers of effort or information that is no longer fit for purpose, such as legacy steps, redundant reviews or 'just in case' processes that linger out of habit, not utility.

- **Overprocessing.** When the attempt to make something robust ends up making it unreadable, unmovable or unworkable.

Sometimes, noise feels like safety, as if we're being responsible and covering our bases. But really we're slowing ourselves down with false signals and padded systems. We end up managing the process instead of making the progress.

This is what Red Brick Thinking calls the *interference layer* — the build-up of inputs, obligations and artefacts that no longer sharpen the work, but instead smother it. The interference layer is the static between what we want to say and what actually gets heard: the friction between what matters and what moves.

CLEAR SPACE TO CUT THROUGH THE NOISE

Not all noise is loud. Some of it wears a lanyard, sends calendar invites and calls itself *best practice*.

We were sitting in a café, halfway through our second cuppas, when my friend, fellow author and cognitive overload expert Lynne Cazaly, dropped the kind of line that makes you stop mid-sip.

'You know what people need to stop doing to manage cognitive overload?' she said. 'Believing someone's coming to save them from it.'

She wasn't being dramatic. Just clear.

She went on to say that we act like the problem is temporary, as if once our tech stack syncs properly, AI improves a bit more or someone finally invents the perfect productivity system, we'll be rescued from the mess in our heads. But it doesn't work that way. 'Cognitive load is human,' she said. 'It's our responsibility. Some people might be working and listening to a podcast, or in a meeting and checking emails. This kind of multitasking really doesn't work—no one is good at it—and it doesn't help us; it makes us feel worse and cope less effectively.'

We hold on to noise because we mistake it for value.

Lynne says that the hardest part is letting go of the idea that you need to hold it all, or even that you *can* hold it all. You can't. That moment when you say, 'No, I won't read that report right now; I'll clear some space first' is a sign you're making a red brick decision. Your brain will thank you for it.

NOISE AS AN AVOIDANCE STRATEGY

Research published in 2017 on busyness as a status symbol found that in today's knowledge economy, people often associate a busy, overextended schedule with higher social status, which is a complete reversal of past eras, where leisure signalled success.

We fill our days with shallow work, perform our productivity and wonder why we feel so tired when we're not making actual progress.

Technology doesn't help, as most tools are designed for engagement, not utility. More notifications equals more time in the app, and more channels equals more attention harvested. We are drowning in features, tabs, dashboards and metrics, and starved of direction.

Platforms thrive on unpredictable rewards. Every ping, like or notification gives us a micro-hit of stimulation and, over time, this conditions our brains to *crave interruption*, even when it costs us focus.

We hold on to noise because it's easier than silence.

People would rather do anything than be alone with their thoughts. A famous 2014 study by Timothy Wilson and his colleagues at the University of Virginia, published in *Science*, found that when people were asked to sit alone in a room with no distractions for 6–15 minutes, with only an electric shock for company, many found it so uncomfortable that they chose to self-administer electric shocks rather than sit in silence.

When we slow down, we're forced to confront harder questions: 'What's essential? What's noise? What have I been avoiding by staying constantly stimulated?'

Noise lets us avoid the discomfort of clarity.

Psychologists like Susan David and Russ Harris have explored how noise and busyness act as *avoidance strategies*. We fill our time and attention to avoid sitting with discomfort, uncertainty, sadness, anxiety or hard decisions.

WHEN EVERYONE IS INVOLVED, NOTHING GETS DONE

Noise has a cost — and we're all paying for it.

At a large distribution centre on the edge of Melbourne, a warehouse team was struggling to meet delivery timeframes. Orders were getting packed late, items were going missing, customers were frustrated and the warehouse staff were exhausted.

From the outside, it looked like a resourcing issue, with too few people and too much demand. But the real strain came from the internal noise, not the number of hands helping.

It wasn't until they brought in key members from across the organisation to solve the problem that they figured out where things were going wrong.

Every morning, the warehouse team would arrive, ready to work, but they couldn't start packing orders until the finance team released them. The finance team, in turn, couldn't release the orders until a new cost centre code was manually entered into the system, a process introduced six months earlier to 'improve accountability'. Only two people were authorised to enter that code, and they worked part-time.

Meanwhile, the sales team, completely unaware of the bottleneck, kept promising customers same-day dispatch, confident that the warehouse could deliver. Technically, it could; but operationally, the staff were stuck.

Boxes piled up, staff clocked overtime, morale dropped and customers who'd paid for fast shipping were left wondering why their orders hadn't even left the building.

It didn't take long to figure out this wasn't a people problem. It wasn't even a process problem in isolation. It was noise in the form of interference — which came from an internal system built for internal comfort, not external coherence. Each department had good intentions, but the lack of alignment created resistance. Layers of sign-off, approvals and coding rules meant the work moved slowly, even when people were working fast.

By the time the noise was traced, named and resolved, the damage had already been done. Customers had gone elsewhere, refunds were being issued and the warehouse team, who were closest to the customer experience, carried the blame for a breakdown they didn't cause.

That's the cost of noise: not just delays, but disconnection between teams, systems, promises and delivery.

In this case, fixing the problem involved subtracting the unnecessary steps that protected the process but punished the outcome.

Noise burns decision-making energy on things that don't matter. It slows projects through loops of unnecessary feedback and fills our days with motion instead of meaning. We end up drained, distracted and disoriented — not because we're lazy, but because we're overloaded.

In teams, noise kills ownership. When everyone's across everything, no one's truly accountable for anything. Strategy becomes vague, priorities blur and performance suffers, even when everyone is working hard.

At an individual level, noise fractures focus. It pulls us into hyper-responsiveness and away from deep, meaningful work. We check things off but rarely feel clear. We're informed but not aligned; busy, but not effective.

Noise stops us from hearing what matters most.

WHEN GOOD SYSTEMS SLOW GREAT WORK

There are no loud sirens: noise shows up quietly in the extra step, the missed cue and the work that feels heavier than it should. It often feels like momentum, until everything slows down.

- **You feel it the moment you open your laptop.** Before you've even started, you already feel behind, as if the day began without you and you're scrambling to catch up.

- **Your calendar is full, but your priorities are blurry.** The time is accounted for, but the focus is missing. Meetings are stacked back to back but there's no real sense of what matters most.

- **You feel flat out every day but can't point to what's actually moving.** You're working hard, reacting constantly, but the real progress is hard to find — and even harder to measure.

- **You notice that everyone's tagged, copied in and 'kept in the loop', but when it comes time to make a decision, no one owns it.** The more people who become involved, the less clear the accountability is.

- **You see a flurry of activity across your team, chats, tasks and check-ins, but you're unsure whether any of**

this activity is moving things forward. There's motion, but not momentum.

- **You catch yourself toggling endlessly — email, message, socials, headlines.** You're consuming, reacting and responding, but you haven't absorbed a thing.

- **You hear yourself saying, 'Let's keep it, just in case.'** You hold on out of habit rather than usefulness and, slowly, clutter becomes culture.

When everything demands your attention, nothing gets your *full* attention. Certainty will only come from subtracting the noise that offers no clear benefit.

WHEN BEST PRACTICE ISN'T WHAT'S BEST

In the Netherlands, the healthcare system was transformed when a small home-care organisation called Buurtzorg threw out one of the most entrenched 'best practices' in medicine: top-down control.

The organisation scrapped layers of management and gave small nursing teams full autonomy. There were no complex scheduling systems and no heavy oversight, just well-trained professionals trusted to care for their patients however they saw fit.

The outcome was better care, happier staff and lower costs.

This approach, known in healthcare circles as *de-implementation*, identifies what no longer works and lets it go. It is not a reckless or reactive approach; instead, it is thoughtful and strategic.

In education, Peter M DeWitt makes the same case in his book *De-implementation: Creating the Space to Focus on What Works*. Schools are often overloaded with programs, assessments, reporting tools and strategies, each one added with good intent, but when put together, they become noise.

DeWitt calls for discipline to help reduce workload and reclaim clarity. He supports the idea of planned, purposeful abandonment.

This is the quiet power of strategic subtraction. It doesn't always feel heroic and it rarely makes headlines, but in systems built on overload, removing what no longer adds value is one of the boldest, most useful things we can do.

Noise isn't neutral. It steals time, energy and focus, and unless we actively reduce it, it grows.

CUT THE CLUTTER; KEEP THE CORE

In the early 1980s, an Australian doctor and biomedical engineer named Graeme Clark set out to solve a problem that most people thought was impossible: how to restore hearing to people with profound deafness.

At the time, the very idea of implanting an electronic device into the human ear was seen as dangerous and delusional. The inner ear is one of the most intricate, delicate systems in the human body, and any disruption risked making things worse. But Clark had a reason to try. His own father had suffered from hearing loss, and he'd seen firsthand the impact of this.

So he went to work, with the intention not just to build a device, but to build a bridge back into sound.

What emerged would eventually become Cochlear Limited, a global company and one of Australia's most iconic success stories. And this breakthrough didn't come from scale, flashy tech or over-engineered prototypes, it came from eliminating interference.

Early versions of cochlear implants were complex and overcrowded: dozens of electrodes firing signals, bulky processors adding weight, clunky controls introducing friction.

The goal was noble — if we can't recreate hearing perfectly, let's simulate as much of it as possible — but the strategy backfired, and all it delivered was confusion. People didn't need *more* sound, they needed the *right* sound: speech, connection and comprehension.

So, the team at Cochlear flipped the question from 'What else can we add?' to 'What's interfering with the outcome?'

They removed the excess electrodes that muddied the signal, streamlined the hardware, refined the signal path and stripped away the interface clutter. Every layer removed brought the user closer to what mattered.

They weren't just building a device — they were removing everything that got in the way of its purpose.

Letting go of noise is about returning to clarity, coherence and calm. But if it were easy, we'd have done it already.

The hardest part isn't identifying what's noisy; it's untangling our sense of worth from the noise itself. We've spent years proving our value through presence, speed and responsiveness. Letting go of noise can feel like letting go of proof.

Real impact comes from knowing where you stand and making space around that. When you release what no longer sharpens your signal, you work better, lead better, live better and listen more deeply.

Start small. Archive the dashboard you haven't checked in months. Leave the thread that spirals but never lands. Say no to the meeting that exists only out of routine. You'll feel the silence at first, but then you'll appreciate the relief.

Removing noise is an act of discipline. It says, 'I know what matters here, I know what gets in the way and I'm not afraid to subtract.'

Pay attention to where you are checking out instead of checking in. Ask yourself, 'Where are decisions slow, and why? Is it because too many people are involved, or nothing is clear?'

You don't need to be across everything. You need to act on purpose.

And it starts with silence.

Chapter 12
Stimulation

In late 2023, a new kind of traveller started popping up on social media — not plugged into a podcast, not watching a movie, not even sipping a coffee. Just… sitting. Eyes forward, mind untethered, tray table up. This was 'rawdogging' a flight: flying without distractions, entertainment or even headphones.

The phrase began circulating on TikTok, often paired with grainy selfies and captions like 'rawdogging this flight — no snacks, no shows, just me and my thoughts'.

But beneath the jokes was something real: a growing curiosity, maybe even hunger, for stillness. For being fully, and uncomfortably, present. Thousands of people began sharing their own rawdogging moments, turning a viral meme into a surprisingly resonant message: perhaps we don't always need more stimulation.

The image of someone voluntarily enduring a long-haul flight without stimulation — just sitting there, alone with their thoughts — felt both absurd and strangely heroic. People laughed at the meme, shared it and nodded in quiet recognition. We knew exactly what this meant.

Rawdogging didn't start as a mindfulness trend. It began, unapologetically, as crude sexual slang — specifically, for having sex without a condom. No protection, no buffer, just, well... raw. It was graphic, provocative and, for a long time, unusable outside certain conversations.

Like all language, it evolved, slipping into casual speech and crossing into meme culture. And somewhere along the way, it became something else entirely.

Today, to *rawdog* something means to go through it completely unbuffered. No playlist, no coffee, no scroll, no support system — just you and the thing you're doing, exactly as it is.

It's been applied to everything from meetings to morning commutes, from gym sessions to airline travel. You're not just doing the thing; you're doing it *raw.*

What started as a joke revealed something deeper: we've become so dependent on constant stimulation that *doing nothing* now counts as meme-worthy.

Even outside the plane, it's catching on. People talk about rawdogging their day: waking up and going to work with no caffeine, no social scroll and no morning ritual, just sheer willpower and vibes. They talk about rawdogging sleep, rawdogging their to-do list, rawdogging life itself.

LIFE ON THE FEED: THE AGE OF ALWAYS ON

We are deep in the age of dopamine saturation. Every scroll, ping, like, tab, sip, swipe, purchase and reply delivers a micro-hit. Harmless, maybe, but definitely relentless, and together, these hits keep our brains in a near-constant state of seeking, scanning and craving. We've trained ourselves to flinch towards stimulation the moment space appears.

- Standing in a line? Phone.

- Commercial break? TikTok.

- Microwave timer? Instagram.

- Moment of discomfort? Something sweet, something numbing, something *else*.

What looks like weakness is actually our wiring. Dopamine drives anticipation, not pleasure, and modern life is engineered to keep us in a state of near satisfaction, constantly reaching for the next hit. We're always just one more scroll, one more refresh, one more bite, one more … *something* away.

We're never quite still and never quite present.

That's what makes things like 'rawdogging' flights, walks or Mondays so oddly meaningful. Behind the absurdity is a small act of mutiny: a refusal to be constantly fed. A choice to sit with the itch, rather than scratch it. A chance to feel what's *actually* there when you stop buffering every moment with input.

We used to look things up. When I was a kid (dare I say it, 'in the olden days') we had a set of *Encyclopedia Brittanica*. Whenever we were curious, or lacking in knowledge about something, Dad would always go to the encyclopedia for the answer. Provided the question was related to something pre-1964, we were safe.

Now we scroll until something finds us.

This is the shift: from active seeking to passive absorbing; from 'What do I want to know?' to 'What does the algorithm want to show me today?' We don't open our phones with a question — we open them with boredom, and let the feed fill the silence.

And it never stops.

The scroll is infinite, the feed is always updating, the content never sleeps — and neither, it seems, do we.

We live in an age where we're always on, always available, always updating, always taking in more than we can possibly process:

- We consume while walking, talking, eating, commuting and even in the bathroom.
- We queue up podcasts for the shower.
- We watch cooking videos we'll never replicate.
- We save workouts we'll never do.
- We read advice we'll forget within minutes.

It's content as ambient noise and attention as autopilot.

Modern life is a multi-tab experience, and our brains rarely have the chance to close one loop before a dozen more open. We skim-read and start things we never finish, and when we do have a moment of pause — standing in line, waiting for a friend, boiling water — we flinch. Not out of need, but out of habit. Reach for the phone, refresh the feed and buffer the stillness.

The idea of sitting with nothing is unimaginable. Unbearable, even.

But it wasn't always this way.

There was a time, not that long ago, when we were bored on a regular basis. Long car rides, waiting rooms, airport lounges, and childhood afternoons with no plans and no screens — and in that boredom lived imagination, play, daydreaming, doodling, wondering and real rest.

My family frequently did the Sydney-to-Melbourne drive, travelling the full stretch of the Hume Highway long before rest stops were curated and car interiors were packed with screens.

We lived in Sydney and my mum's family lived in Melbourne, so every school holidays we'd pile into the car with no devices, no itinerary, no curated playlists or snack boxes divided by hour. We'd just *go*. And back then, that trip could take up to 12 hours.

Here's what stands out to me now: my parents never once planned for our boredom.

Sometimes we'd sing along to the radio, play I-Spy or track the alphabet on number plates. Sometimes we'd stare out the window for what felt like forever, watching the landscape change in slow motion and dozing off for an hour or so. There were no colouring books, no screens and no Pinterest-approved backseat activities, and the only stops were for fuel, food and toilets.

The journey took over. That's how Mum put it years later: 'The trip just took over.'

Nowadays, that idea feels strange. *Letting the trip take over.* Letting space expand without needing to fill it. Letting boredom arrive without rushing to cure it.

Boredom used to be a feature of the journey, not the result of a lack of planning, and in those long stretches of nothing, our minds wandered, connected, rested and imagined. Without knowing it, we were making space for thought, for presence, for simply being. We were *rawdogging.*

Today, boredom is treated like a glitch — something to fix or a sign of a missed opportunity. We've so completely erased the gap between stimulus and response that even a few seconds of emptiness makes us twitch.

Stimulation is no longer an exception; it's the default.

Every ping, scroll, ping again cycle creates a feedback loop of anticipation: not necessarily for pleasure, just the promise of *something.* Something new, more or else. And when it's available at all times, it's no longer a choice — it's a reflex.

- We check, not because we're curious, but because we're trained to.

- We scroll, not because we're learning, but because we're restless.

- We consume, not because it feeds us, but because silence now feels unfamiliar.

That's the real cost of being always on: not just fragmented attention, but frayed presence. We're rarely where we are. Our bodies are here, but our attention is one step ahead, or five steps sideways.

And the irony is we're doing all this to feel connected — but often, it's the very thing pulling us further from ourselves.

THE FEED DISORIENTS

Social media feeds flood us with so much, so fast, so often that we forget how to hear our own thoughts, and we forget how to finish them. We forget what it feels like to arrive at an idea slowly — through stillness, not stimulus — and in that forgetting, we lose something fundamental: the ability to be alone with ourselves without reaching for a buffer.

Once you see it, once you feel how deeply this culture of 'always on' has embedded itself into your rhythms, you can begin to question it.

Life on the feed is constant input. It's time to reclaim your space from the scroll, your calm from the chaos and your attention from the endless loop of 'just one more'.

ADDICTED TO ANTICIPATION

We often confuse dopamine with pleasure. But dopamine isn't the reward. It's the chase.

Neuroscientist Robert Sapolsky and others have shown that dopamine is not triggered primarily by the reward itself; it spikes most in anticipation of the reward. Once the reward arrives, dopamine levels actually drop.

This makes dopamine a *motivational* chemical, not a happiness one. It's what keeps us seeking, checking and scrolling — not because it feels good, but because it *might*.

This is why modern life feels so full, yet so hollow. Every ping, scroll, click and swipe is stringing us along.

And we feel it:

- The restless energy that shows up in moments that used to be still

- The inability to sit through a TV show without checking your phone

- The way you open a new tab before the last one finishes loading

- The strange, nameless anxiety that creeps in whenever there's space.

This restlessness aligns with research by psychiatrist Anna Lembke, author of *Dopamine Nation*, who found that our constant search for stimulation leads to a dopamine imbalance — where even small moments of quiet can feel like withdrawal.

In her book, Lembke makes a confronting comparison, saying, 'The smartphone is the modern-day hypodermic needle, delivering digital dopamine 24/7 for a wired generation.'

This is also supported by technology ethicist Tristan Harris, formerly at Google, who's spoken widely about how modern tech environments are engineered to turn our attention into a commodity, keeping us in a loop of compulsive anticipation.

We aren't chasing joy; we're chasing relief from discomfort. On a 2023 episode of the American Psychological Association podcast *Speaking of Psychology*, psychiatrist Daniel Lieberman and writer Michael Long argue that dopamine is tied more to future-oriented desire than present-moment pleasure. We use dopamine-seeking behaviours not to feel joy, but to escape discomfort or boredom.

Dopamine used to help us forage, hunt and seek, but in today's environment it's being hijacked — not by accident but by design. Platforms, products and notifications are engineered to keep our reward system on a tight loop of tiny hits, with just enough satisfaction to keep you coming back and never enough to let you leave.

WHEN EVERYTHING GRABS YOU, NOTHING GROUNDS YOU

After years of feeling his focus unravel, checking emails mid-conversation, losing hours to rabbit holes and forgetting books he'd just read, Johann Hari realised he wasn't just distracted, he was *wired* for distraction. So, he tried an experiment.

Hari booked a remote cottage in Provincetown, Massachusetts, and cut himself off: no phone, no Wi-Fi, no social media, no emails. Just notebooks, books, silence and space.

And for the first few days, he was miserable.

His brain, so used to being fed, began to protest. He paced, he fidgeted, craving something, anything, to fill the void. But slowly, something shifted. His thoughts became clearer, his ability to concentrate returned and his mind felt slower, but in the best possible way: less reactive and more intentional.

He later described it as 'coming back to myself'.

But Hari didn't stop at personal insight; he zoomed out.

In *Stolen Focus*, he outlines 12 causes of our attention crisis, and not all of them involve screens. Many are cultural, environmental and hidden in plain sight: sleep deprivation, food, pollution, overstimulation and, perhaps most poignantly, the way we raise children.

He writes about how attention is not just a personality trait but a skill — and like all skills, it has to be practised, stretched and protected.

Kids today are growing up in environments where deep play, imagination and boredom have been systematically erased. Every moment is structured, every silence is filled and every instance of discomfort is resolved with a screen, a snack, a stimulus.

'We are now raising our children in a context where they are being constantly interrupted, constantly surveilled, and constantly tracked,' Hari writes. 'What we've lost is not just focus, but the freedom that made focus possible.'

That freedom — the ability to get lost in something, to build a fort, to draw for hours, to daydream — is neurological. It's how we build the mental muscle of sustained attention.

Adults aren't exempt. We, too, now live in fragmented time that's sliced into pings and check-ins and half-completed thoughts.

We don't live in hours anymore — we live in moments of almost-doing-something and, over time, it is our focus that suffers, as well as our sense of presence.

Red Brick Thinking isn't in the business of assigning blame. It simply asks:

- What would happen if I let the itch stay itchy?

- What might I notice if I didn't feed it immediately?

- What could return to me, if I gave myself space to feel bored?

Because that's where real attention lives: not in the stimulation, but in the silence that follows. Your attention is buried beneath the anticipation and is waiting for you to stop chasing, so it can finally settle in.

And if you're willing to sit with the silence, if only for a minute, you might just hear it again.

WHEN STILLNESS FEELS UNBEARABLE

The Red Brick of Stimulation arrives unannounced, as a slow loss — a kind of mental and emotional blurring.

- **Your hand reaches for your phone before your feet touch the floor.** Not out of urgency, but out of habit. It's as if you can't start the day without filling the stillness of the morning with activity.

- **You catch it during downtime.** A show plays on the television while you scroll through something else. It's entertainment layered with distraction, because one stream of stimulation no longer feels like enough.

- **You open five tabs with good intentions, only to forget what the first one was for.** Your mind is scattered across digital breadcrumbs — constantly jumping, rarely landing.

- **You feel both exhausted and wired.** Your body's tired, and your brain's still buzzing, like you're too full to rest, but too flat to focus. Restlessness is dressed up as productivity.

- **You say you crave quiet but find ways to avoid it the second it arrives.** You fill the silence with podcasts, reels and news. Anything but stillness.

- **You check notifications with a kind of urgency that doesn't match what's waiting.** It's a reflex more than a decision.

- **You wonder what happened to your attention span.** You used to sit still for longer, read deeper, think in complete thoughts. You haven't lost your focus; you've just trained it to jump.

This is the nervous system in overdrive — not from danger, but from design.

We tell ourselves it's just one more scroll, one more video, one more tab, one more message, one more little reward … but dopamine is like a breadcrumb trail, with each hit leading you deeper down the rabbit hole.

And content — beautiful, infinite, optimised content — is designed to keep that loop alive.

That's the myth of 'just one more': that you're in control; that you're choosing what to watch, click and consume. But often, we don't choose — we drift. We scroll through boredom, anxiety or avoidance until 30 minutes vanish into a timeline you barely remember entering.

The worst part is that much of it *is* good content — entertaining, insightful and addictively efficient. There are of course memes and outrage, and there are also plenty of life hacks, brilliant podcasts, calming videos, recipes, creativity and beauty — and that's what makes it so slippery.

It feels useful and justifiable.

Make no mistake, this is a business model. Attention is the economy, your brain is the currency and 'just one more' is the slogan of an industry that profits from your pause never arriving.

In 2013, while working as a design ethicist at Google, Tristan Harris authored a presentation titled 'A call to minimise distraction and respect users' attention'. He highlighted how tech platforms exploit human psychology to keep users engaged, often at the expense of their wellbeing. His insights sparked internal discussions at Google and led him to co-found the Center for Humane Technology in 2018, aiming to realign technology with humanity's best interests.

Harris's advocacy sheds light on how design choices in apps and platforms, like infinite scroll and push notifications, are crafted to hijack our attention. These features create a cycle where 'just one more' becomes an endless loop, making it challenging to disconnect.

Red Brick Thinking doesn't demonise content, but it does question the compulsion:

- Is this nourishing me or numbing me?
- Am I choosing this, or avoiding something else?
- What would I have done with this hour, if I hadn't been in a trance?

Because every moment you're watching someone else's life, you're not living your own.

This isn't a guilt trip; it's a pattern interruption.

Red Brick Thinking is the quiet voice that says, 'You can stop now, you're already full.'

LIVING WITH BOREDOM

Boredom was never the problem. It's just the space between inputs, but we've forgotten what to do with it.

In an age of instant distraction, boredom feels unbearable, like sitting in a room that's too quiet, too empty, too still. But boredom is also the birthplace of imagination. It's where new ideas start to breathe — where your mind stops reacting and starts inventing, and where things you didn't know you were feeling start to surface.

Boredom forces the mind inwards.

It lets things rise and connect, so you can imagine things that don't yet exist because you're not trying to escape the now.

The red brick lesson here isn't to be bored for the sake of it; it's to stop medicating every moment of mental discomfort with a screen, a scroll, a snack or a hit of something else. Boredom isn't the enemy here: beneath boredom is imagination, beneath imagination is desire, and beneath desire is truth.

When you buffer every moment with content, you don't just lose time. You also lose access to what might've arrived in its place:

- The next great idea

- The real reason you feel stuck

- A memory you need to process, a thought you need to write down, a feeling you don't realise you're carrying.

Some call it dopamine fasting, while others call it boredom tolerance. I call it Red Brick Thinking. Maybe it's simply remembering how to be human without a layer of noise between us and our lives.

In an age of constant digital stimulation, we've stopped treating attention as something we own and started treating it like public property. Anyone with a ping, a platform or a push notification can reach in and grab it. We give our attention away, often without realising it. According to research highlighted in *Fast Company*, the average attention span on a digital screen plummeted from 2.5 minutes in 2004 to just 47 seconds in 2020. We've internalised that interruption is normal as we flit, we scroll, we refresh — not because it's valuable, but because it's available.

But attention is not infinite, passive or neutral. It's what you build your life out of.

What you give attention to, you give energy to, and what you give energy to, you become.

That's why Red Brick Thinking treats attention as sacred: not precious in a fragile way, but powerful in a generative way. When you begin to reclaim your attention, you're choosing what gets to shape you.

In a world addicted to attention-grabbing, your attention is no longer just a habit. It's a vote, it's a boundary, it's a resource — and it's yours to reclaim.

This isn't a manifesto for monk mode. You don't need to delete your accounts, move to the bush or turn your phone into a brick. Modern life runs on connection, and it's where we find news, humour, friendship, creativity, beauty and belonging.

The feed isn't the enemy. It's our relationship to the constant stimulation that's worth rethinking, because the goal isn't to quit everything — it's to stop letting everything in.

Change the input and everything recalibrates.

Chapter 13

Urgency

When you walk into Rick Rubin's Malibu music studio, Shangri-La, there's an immediate sense that time is behaving differently.

There are no countdown timers, clocks on the walls or whiteboards scribbled with deadlines: just natural light, open space and the quiet hum of possibility.

Rubin, one of the most influential music producers of the past four decades, has shaped iconic albums with artists like Adele, Johnny Cash, the Red Hot Chili Peppers and Ed Sheeran. But unlike the high-pressure environments often associated with the music industry, Rubin has built a studio deliberately stripped of urgency.

As revealed in the Showtime documentary series *Shangri-La*, Rubin's approach is subtle but powerful: he removes pressure from the process. Artists arrive when they're ready, and sessions unfold without rigid timelines. The emphasis isn't on squeezing productivity into the day — it's on creating the right conditions for meaningful work to emerge.

Rubin trusts that when the distractions fall away and the pressure lifts, something better comes through. He is known not for imposing a particular sound, but for stripping things back to help artists find the emotional and creative core of their work.

Shangri-La is a sanctuary in a world that worships urgency.

THE ILLUSION OF NOW

The Red Brick of Urgency is the pressure to act fast, regardless of whether fast is needed, helpful or even possible. It creeps into our calendars, our inboxes and our team cultures. It presents every task as a fire, every request as a priority and every interruption as justified.

It's easy to mistake this pressure for momentum because urgency mimics productivity. It creates motion and generates heat. But heat isn't the same as progress, and motion won't always lead in the right direction.

This red brick hums in the periphery, showing up in subject lines marked 'urgent', in meeting invites with no breathing room between them and in the constant expectation of immediate replies. We absorb it into our working rhythm until it *becomes* the rhythm — and once urgency becomes normal, calm starts to feel like laziness.

We don't set out to build urgency into our systems, but it happens all the same. It happens when we fail to plan far enough ahead, when we default to instant messaging without boundaries, and when leadership rewards speed more visibly than thoughtfulness.

Over time, urgency shifts from being a tool we occasionally use to a culture we unconsciously follow. It stops being a response to a genuine crisis and starts becoming the operating system. When everything feels urgent, we lose the ability to see what's truly important.

This red brick is particularly deceptive because it feels useful. It energises teams, keeps the pace up and makes people look busy, but it's a short-term thrill with long-term costs. Urgency is often a symptom of poor structure, unclear priorities and overwhelmed capacity.

THE COMFORT OF CONSTANT MOTION

We hold on to urgency because it flatters us.

It makes us feel needed, important, in demand. When the pace is fast and the stakes feel high, we can mistake stress for significance. Researchers call this the 'urgency effect', a cognitive bias that leads people to prioritise time-sensitive tasks over more important but less urgent ones, simply because the deadline feels immediate.

In a 2018 study published in *Journal of Consumer Research*, researchers found that people disproportionately focus on urgent tasks, even when those tasks offer less value, due to a psychological pull towards time-bound activity.

Urgency is also seductive because it offers clarity. When everything feels urgent, you don't have to make hard choices about what matters most. You just respond, act and move. There's comfort in that momentum as it spares us the discomfort of pausing to think strategically or say no.

The team member who replies at 11pm is praised for commitment. The one who blocks out time to think is seen as unavailable. The result is that we absorb urgency not just as a habit, but as an identity. 'I work fast' becomes code for 'I matter.'

There's also the fear of being left out, left behind or seen as less valuable. We fear that if we slow down, we'll fall short. Urgency lets us stay ahead of that fear — or at least distract ourselves from it.

Urgency removes the need for discipline, planning and boundaries. It keeps us reactive, which feels easier in the moment than being intentional. We don't have to decide what deserves our time; we just respond to whatever's shouting loudest.

We become skilled at moving quickly, but not necessarily at moving well. Letting go of urgency feels risky, until we realise how much it's been costing us all along.

ALWAYS ON — ALWAYS OFF TRACK

Urgency promises momentum but delivers depletion.

When urgency becomes the default, not the exception, the quality of everything suffers — our thinking, our focus, our relationships and our leadership. It turns our work into a series of micro-sprints that never end and, over time, that kind of responsiveness comes at a steep price.

When we're always rushing to the next thing, we don't leave room for reflection. Strategic thinking shrinks, and decisions are made hastily. We move fast but in circles.

Urgency favours immediate action over intentional direction, which pulls us away from the bigger picture.

A study published in 2008 found that task-switching, often caused by urgent interruptions, costs us an average of 23 minutes. In other words, it takes 23 minutes to regain full concentration. That's a drain on cognitive energy that compounds throughout the day. Each ping, each 'got a minute?', each unexpected call fragments our attention and leaves us more exhausted than the work itself.

Leaders caught in constant urgency don't lead—they react. They default to putting out fires instead of preventing them. Team members start modelling the same behaviour, creating a culture where thoughtfulness is replaced by speed, and responsiveness is mistaken for effectiveness.

There's also a deeper, more subtle cost: we begin to confuse *busy* with *valuable*. The faster we go, the more we lose touch with the difference between activity and impact. Our days become full, but not full of progress. That's how teams burn out without actually getting better.

And the toll isn't just professional. Constant urgency bleeds into our evenings, our weekends, our relationships. It robs us of presence and rest, as well as the space where our best thinking and most human conversations happen. When the pressure to be 'on' never stops, neither does the tension.

Urgency is unsustainable. We end the day drained—not because we did too much, but because we never stopped to do the right things.

One of my coaching clients, Maya, was leading a fast-growing tech business when she came to me with a problem she couldn't quite name.

The numbers were strong and the team was smart, but the pace was unsustainable. Every conversation buzzed with urgency. Emails flew around at all hours, and meetings were stacked from morning to evening. Decisions were made on the fly and, despite all the hustle, no one felt ahead of the game.

'I feel like we're racing all the time,' she told me. 'But I'm not sure we're actually getting anywhere.'

Maya made a decision that turned heads...she cancelled Mondays.

Not just meetings. *Everything.* No launches, catch-ups or reviews. Mondays became thinking days. A quiet, protected space for reflection, strategy and preparation. Her only message to the team? 'Use it to get ahead, not to catch up.'

The pushback came fast: 'We're already under pressure.' 'We don't have time for this.' 'What will people think?'

But Maya held her ground.

Three months later, the difference was undeniable. Midweek energy improved, last-minute fire fights decreased and project timelines stabilised. The team began working better and thinking better, and the unexpected result was that they were working faster than ever before.

THE PACE THAT OWNS YOU

Urgency sneaks in disguised as diligence and drive embedding itself in your calendar, your language and your leadership defaults. Before long, rushing becomes routine, and stillness feels suspicious. You're busy, responsive, in demand and completely untethered from what actually matters.

- **You open your laptop and your heart rate picks up.** You're not alarmed by what's there so much as the thought of what *might* be there.

- **You say yes before checking your calendar.** Somehow, pausing feels riskier than overcommitting.

- **You tell yourself, 'I'll just get this one thing done first.'** Before you know it, that one thing has become 10, and the important work isn't happening at all.

- **You find yourself replying to messages at red lights, in queues or while brushing your teeth.** Replying later feels like a luxury you can't afford.

- **You notice that even short pauses feel uncomfortable.** A slow moment makes you reach for your phone, not your thoughts.

- **You've stopped asking, 'Does this need to be done?'** Instead, you only ask, 'How fast can I get it off my plate?'

- **You feel edgy during downtime.** You have a sense something's wrong when nothing is wrong.

- **You keep chasing inbox zero, calendar control and clean slates.** But these clean slates never last. The urgency resets faster than you can catch your breath.

You say things like 'I just want to get ahead' or 'I work better under pressure', but deep down you know you're running on fumes, not flow.

You don't need an emergency to feel urgency. It is a culture that never stops moving.

ASSUMPTIONS OF UNREASONABLENESS

Urgency is a script, not a truth.

Saying no to it is like rewriting the existing script that says you need to answer everything immediately, you can't question the deadline and you'll be seen as difficult if you dare to ask, 'When do you actually need this?'

We carry these unspoken beliefs like rules: that we must always be available, always be fast, always be agreeable. But these are unreasonable assumptions, driven by the quiet fear that if we ask for space, we'll be seen as lazy; if we explain our priorities, we'll be seen as disloyal; and if we set a boundary, we'll be seen as selfish.

So, we don't ask or check.

Letting go of urgency begins when we start trusting a different assumption: *reasonableness*, the belief that most people can handle questioning and are capable of hearing 'Not yet,' 'I need until Thursday' or 'This isn't the top priority right now.' And if they can't? That's not about your boundary—it's about their expectation.

Resisting urgency helps us think better, lead more clearly and move from panic to presence. Sometimes the most strategic thing you can do is to stop, breathe and question the pace.

I caught up with productivity expert and CEO of Adapt Productivity, Dermot Crowley, recently, and we got talking about urgency — specifically, the cost of constantly being in 'go mode'.

He made a point that really stuck with me: some urgency is real and unavoidable, but most of it is manufactured. Often, we create our own pressure by leaving things too late. Or we inherit someone else's poor planning, and suddenly their emergency becomes our responsibility.

According to Dermot, when teams or organisations are always operating in urgency mode, it becomes a kind of cultural norm. No one gets pulled up for last-minute scrambles — they're almost expected. The result is a constant cycle of stress, a decline in the quality of the work and a team that's reactive instead of focused on what truly matters.

He offered a mindset shift that's deceptively simple but powerful: responsiveness versus reactivity.

He said, 'When we're responsive, we act with intention. When we're reactive, we just ... react. We skip the thinking part.'

Dermot likened it to how we teach kids to cross the road: Stop, Look, Listen. That basic rule provides a solid guide for how to respond to challenges at work: Slow down. Pause. Think. *Then* act. Not every ping, call or crisis deserves an instant reaction.

'The tortoise wins the race,' he reminded me. And in a world obsessed with speed, that's not just a children's fable — it's a productivity principle.

Some deadlines are fixed, such as flight times, live broadcasts and surgical procedures. The rest are mostly fiction.

We tell ourselves the proposal *has* to be done by 5pm, that inbox zero *must* happen before Friday, that the report *must* be sent before we go on leave. But what we're often reacting to isn't a real constraint, it's an emotional one: a craving for closure, control or the illusion of being on top of things.

These artificial endpoints generate real pressure. We scramble to achieve a task because we've quietly assigned it an urgency that says we need to feel in control of the chaos.

We rush when we could reflect, we prioritise what's immediate over what's important, and we trade depth for speed.

Red Brick Thinking invites a different kind of deadline: one that's driven by purpose, not panic. Ask yourself: Who decided this was the finish line? What happens if it moves? What matters more — that it's done *fast*, or that it's done *well*?

You are not your response time or your output speed. You are allowed to be thoughtful, even in a world that rewards fast.

Let urgency pass. You don't have to chase it.

PART 4

EMOTIONAL RED BRICKS

Some red bricks don't live in our calendars or systems; they live in our hearts.

Emotional Red Bricks are the weight we carry when we put others' needs before our own: when we say yes to avoid guilt, or when we stay too long in roles, routines or relationships that no longer fit. These bricks aren't always visible, but they are felt. Deeply.

We inherit them from traditions, family and the stories we tell ourselves about what it means to be a good person, a hard worker and a reliable friend. Because they're emotional, they're tricky to name — and even harder to set down.

This part of the book surfaces the five Emotional Red Bricks that quietly shape our decisions:

- Weight
- Reactivity
- Overcommitment
- Obligation
- Relationships.

If you've ever felt stretched thin, stuck or quietly resentful, you've probably been carrying a few of these.

Chapter 14

Weight

In 1980, Ferrari was losing. Badly.

Its Formula 1 cars were powerful — but not powerful enough. The instinctive solution was to add more horsepower, bigger engines, more speed and more technology. But no matter how much raw power Ferrari stacked into its cars, it kept losing to smaller, more agile competitors.

Then, in 1981, Ferrari made a radical decision. Instead of adding more, the company asked a different question: 'What's slowing us down?'

The answer was *weight*.

Ferrari's engineers realised that raw power wasn't enough if its cars were too heavy and aerodynamically inefficient. Instead of continuing the arms race for bigger, faster engines, it removed excess weight, stripped away unnecessary components and re-engineered its cars' aerodynamics. Ferrari made the decision to focus on efficiency rather than seeking more brute force.

The result was the Ferrari 126C, the team's first turbocharged Formula 1 car. The early version of the car was difficult to drive and unreliable, but Ferrari persisted. It refined the design, cutting weight and optimising airflow to ensure that the power was being used in the most effective way possible. By removing rather than adding, Ferrari transformed its fortunes.

In 1982 and 1983, Ferrari won back-to-back Constructors' Championships. Its strategy of subtraction had proven itself. It hadn't won by simply piling on more power; it had won by removing what was slowing its cars down.

Look around and you'll see the burden of weight everywhere. Businesses create layer upon layer of process and bureaucracy in an attempt to become more efficient, only to find themselves hampered by their own complexity.

Individuals stack their calendars with back-to-back meetings, believing they're being productive, when they're actually drowning in obligations that sap their energy and focus. Leaders push their teams to do more, faster, without realising that they're stretching people so thin that performance suffers.

The Red Brick of Weight is deceptive, because it isn't always visible. Sometimes it's obvious — packed schedules, bloated processes, inboxes that never quit — but often it's emotional, psychological or even energetic.

It can be energetic because it drains you, which impacts your energy. It is the subtle sense of being depleted by something that may not take up much time in your schedule but still saps your energy. Think of it as the background load on your system: the mental clutter, emotional residue or constant low-level stress that leaves you feeling flat or foggy.

WHAT WE CARRY THAT NO ONE SEES

You feel it in the pause before your alarm goes off, in the quiet sigh before you open your laptop, in the invisible effort it takes to keep showing up, smiling and pushing through. It's the weight of responsibility, with no off switch. You feel under pressure to hold it together — for your team, your family, your clients, your children — while you're quietly unravelling on the inside.

This kind of weight seldom looks like you're in crisis. More often it looks like competence, and that's what makes it so heavy.

Maybe it's the project you said yes to out of obligation, the responsibility no one asked you to carry but you picked up anyway, or the version of success you're still chasing, long after it stopped feeling right.

The most alarming thing about this kind of weight is that we get used to it. We normalise the drag and we forget what light feels like.

My client Angela, a brand strategist for a global cosmetics company, knew this well. She had spent years juggling the demands of a high-pressure career with the relentless, often invisible labour of parenting two small children. From the outside, she looked like she was managing. Projects were being delivered, meals were prepared on time and she was present for bedtimes — but inside, something was unravelling.

When she reached out to me in early 2022, Angela found herself in what she now calls a state of 'emotional deadness'. She wasn't angry or crying. She was just … absent. 'I didn't *feel* like being with my kids. I was there, but not really present.'

It was numbness, a kind of slow erosion that felt like neglect: the result of years of performing competence without pause. She hadn't burned out; she had faded out.

Researchers now have a name for this: *parental burnout*. But despite the name, it's not just parents who are impacted by this phenomenon. It happens to carers, leaders and anyone who spends more time managing other people's needs than tending to their own. It happens when you're holding too much for too long, with too little space left to feel any of it.

THE BURDEN THAT BECOMES NORMAL

We don't hold on to weight because we enjoy it. We hold on because somewhere along the way, we were taught that carrying more meant we were doing well:

- That being dependable meant never saying no
- That being committed meant pushing through
- That being strong meant not asking for help.

So, we layer on expectations — some handed to us, some self-imposed — and we keep going, even when we're exhausted and the load has long since stopped making sense.

We tell ourselves we're just being responsible — that this is what grown-ups do, and the rest will come later, once things settle down. But they never do.

When the World Health Organization classified burnout as a workplace phenomenon, it noted that burnout is driven not just by workload but by chronic emotional strain, especially in those who feel a persistent sense of responsibility or a lack of boundaries.

Psychologist Emily Nagoski, in *Burnout: The Secret to Unlocking the Stress Cycle*, describes this as 'human giver syndrome': the compulsion to give, give, give, often without replenishment, especially among women and people-pleasers.

The weight we carry is rarely about tasks. It's emotional, psychological — existential, even. It's the belief that if we stop doing, the world might unravel — or worse, people might see we're not as together as we appear.

The concept of the 'mental load' (originating in gender studies and labour economics) describes the invisible and ongoing cognitive effort it takes to manage not just your own life, but the lives of others. Sociologist Allison Daminger suggests that the weight we carry isn't physical — it's emotional, cognitive and often unrecognised. This is particularly common in caretaking roles and in people socialised to 'keep it together' for others.

Many of us wear our invisible weight like armour. The late-night reports, the extra tasks, the team we quietly manage beyond our job description, the friend we always call back, even when we have nothing left, become our unspoken proof of worth.

But rather than protecting us, that armour just makes it harder for us to move.

We keep carrying because we confuse heaviness with importance. If something feels weighty, we assume it must matter. We assume we're supposed to carry it — and because we're capable, we do.

Social psychologist Brené Brown has extensively documented how many of us internalise the belief that self-worth is tied to productivity, perfection and meeting others' expectations. In *The Gifts of Imperfection*, she describes productivity as a 'dangerous status symbol' and explains how we use busyness to numb discomfort and prove our value.

Organisational psychologist Adam Grant has written about how highly capable people are often overloaded — not because they can't say no, but because others know they're reliable. This leads to a cycle where competence becomes a trap.

Being good at something doesn't mean it's yours to carry forever. Capability is not a reason to carry everything.

Sometimes, the hardest part of letting go isn't the act itself. The harder part is challenging the story underneath it: the one that says stopping is weak, lightness is irresponsible, and choosing rest, space or simplicity mean you'll be letting people down.

This is what makes the Red Brick of Weight so difficult to see, and even harder to release. It disguises itself as duty, strength and reliability, and yet it's quietly eroding the very things we need to thrive: energy, focus and presence.

Holding on is human, but holding on forever is unsustainable.

CRUSHED BY CAPABILITY

The weight becomes part of you, until one day, you can't move like you used to. You can't think clearly, and you find yourself staring at a task you could do blindfolded and feeling paralysed.

You say things like:

- 'I feel heavy.'
- 'It's hard to get going.'
- 'I'm tired, but sleep doesn't fix it.'

This is the drag of your emotional carry-on:

- The grief you never unpacked
- The expectations you never agreed to
- The versions of yourself you've outgrown but keep performing.

Not all weight is yours to carry forever, and not every kind of heaviness means you're broken. Sometimes it just means you've been holding on for too long.

Red Brick Thinking isn't a way to avoid our responsibilities. It gives us the tools to discern which responsibilities are real and to gently lay down the ones that aren't.

Stop measuring strength by what you can hold on to and start measuring it by what you're willing to set down.

WE CONFUSE MOMENTUM WITH OVERLOAD

Some burdens don't arrive all at once. They build slowly, layer by layer, packaged as opportunity.

- **You feel the heaviness before your feet hit the floor.** You wake up already behind, already bracing.

- **You say yes with a smile and feel it land in your stomach like a stone.** It's another thing to carry; another expectation you didn't really have room for.

- **You find yourself dreading the work — not because it's hard, but because it feels heavier than it should.** It's the kind of weight that doesn't show up in a task list but lingers anyway.

- **You keep the tab open, the draft unsent, the meeting invite unspoken about.** Making a decision feels like one more thing you don't have the energy for.

- **You check your calendar and feel the tightness creep in.** Every square is filled. Every hour has been claimed. You have nowhere to breathe, and nowhere to think.

- **You notice the tension in your body.** Your jaw is clenched, your breath is shallow and your shoulders are high, as if you're holding something you forgot to put down.

- **You tell yourself, 'It's just a busy season.'** Deep down, though, you know this isn't seasonal. It's structural.

- **You don't remember the last time things felt light.** All you know is that everything feels like hard work.

You realise that you have allowed this to creep in because of your inability to say no to each request that crosses your path:

- A new project or collaboration that sounds too good to pass up

- A request for help, mentorship or guidance

- An invitation to join a committee, board or leadership group

- A side hustle, extra role or additional responsibility

- A steady stream of meetings, catch-ups and 'quick' asks that chip away at your time.

None of them are heavy on their own, but together they add up.

This is the weight of compounding commitments, when your yes is coming from the right place but the accumulation is beginning to cost you direction, stamina and peace of mind.

WHEN AMBITION BECOMES EXHAUSTION

Born to farmers in Henan province, Li Jianxiong had worked his way up through the ranks through sheer discipline, grit and loyalty to the grind. As a senior marketing director in China's booming tech sector, he was a product of the '996' culture: working 9am to 9pm, six days a week. It was the unofficial badge of the ambitious, and Li wore it proudly.

At first, the pace was thrilling. His success skyrocketed, promotions followed, his name was trusted in his field and every opportunity that came his way felt like confirmation that he was doing it right.

So, he said yes. Again and again and again. Until the system he was sustaining began to quietly hollow him out.

It started with small signs — fatigue he couldn't shake, a short temper, trouble sleeping, a feeling that his brain was full even when he hadn't achieved anything meaningful that day. Eventually, Li couldn't concentrate in meetings. He struggled to make clear decisions; he became reactive, distracted and emotionally flat.

And still, he kept going — because that's what high performers do.

Until the day he couldn't. In 2017, while managing a major media crisis for his employer, he developed insomnia, heart palpitations and a severe rash, which doctors attributed to a weakened immune system caused by chronic stress.

Li eventually stepped away from his role and, after a long period of recovery, began speaking out about China's culture of overwork. In interviews, he's been honest about the psychological toll of endless accumulation, and of what happens when the ability to say yes outpaces your capacity to hold it. He now helps others find what he had to learn the hard way: that overwhelm doesn't begin with the wrong decision. It begins with too many right ones, made without pause.

This is the tyranny of 'I can handle it.' Because when you're smart, resilient and good at getting things done, people will keep asking and you'll keep saying yes — not out of obligation, but out of identity.

But upholding this identity can cause you to lose your grip on where you actually want to go.

Every yes is a weight, and even beautiful weights will slow you down if you never allow space to breathe.

UNRESOLVED TASKS AND UNCLOSED LOOPS

Some things don't look heavy until you try to move forward and realise they're still hooked to you: a half-written report with your name on it, a draft strategy that's been in limbo for months, the team restructure you've been 'getting around to' for a while, the new initiative that launched with a bang and now lives in a document no one opens.

We often think the things that slow us down are visible — meetings, deadlines, back-to-back calls — but some of the most draining weight we carry is mental, invisible and unfinished.

We have open loops in our mind that remind us of the 'shoulds' and 'somedays' that sit just out of view, like browser tabs we'd forgotten were open. We're not actively thinking about them, but they're still drawing power.

Psychologists call this the *Zeigarnik effect*, which is our brain's tendency to fixate on incomplete tasks. It's why cliffhangers work so well in TV shows, and why that unanswered email follows you into your weekend. Your brain wants to close the loop — and when you don't, it keeps checking back in, quietly and relentlessly draining you.

The *size* of the task doesn't matter; it's whether you've closed the loop.

This is the unseen strain on creative energy, decision-making and momentum, and it slows down entire organisations.

In large organisations, weight may not always show up as headcount or bureaucracy. Sometimes it takes the form of zombies. These can be projects, products, services, reports, processes and sometimes even people. They may be initiatives that once had promise but now drift in a state of half-life. They consume budget, attention and team energy, often without delivering any real value — and yet, we keep them alive.

Organisational life creates strong forces that protect zombies. Sunk-cost bias tells us we have invested too much to stop now; hierarchy discourages challenge; and the desire to be seen as a team player pushes people to continue, even when the work no longer aligns with current needs. In these conditions, silence is safer than honesty.

Some organisations have begun to address this pattern by introducing what they call a *zombie project amnesty*. These amnesties are structured opportunities where teams are invited to surface and review projects that have lost traction. People are given permission to say, 'We are still doing this, but we're no longer sure why.' There's no blame or fallout, just a shared commitment to regaining capacity. This practice makes space for tough, necessary conversations and clears the way for work that matters more.

Ending a project that has outlived its purpose is a sign of leadership. It says we are willing to choose focus over inertia, and alignment over politeness. It is an act of respect — for time, energy and the people doing the work.

Not everything unfinished needs to be finished. Some things need to be released.

We assume that letting go of a project or closing a loop is about tidiness, but it's deeper than that. It's the cognitive relief you get from releasing your mind from the low-grade buzz of the unresolved.

Letting go of the Red Brick of Weight is a return to momentum.

You can't create something new if half your energy is still tied up in things you never had the heart to finish or the courage to end.

You weren't meant to carry everything; you were meant to move.

Red Brick Thinking helps you let go of what makes your effort heavier than it needs to be, so you can focus your effort wisely.

So, lighten up already!

Chapter 15

Reactivity

I n 1974, Princess Anne was riding back to Buckingham Palace when a man blocked the car, pulled out a gun, and attempted to kidnap her.

The situation was pure chaos, with shots fired, people injured and a gun pointed directly at the princess. In the midst of it all, Anne didn't scream or panic, and she certainly didn't freeze. She looked at the man demanding she get out of the car and, with terrifying calm, said: 'Not bloody likely.'

That's it.

That moment, strange as it sounds, is a masterclass in presence. No dramatic outburst or terrified breakdown, just a clear refusal delivered with spine and certainty.

That's the point here. Not necessarily how to handle hostage situations, but resisting the instinct to react, lash out, escalate or jump in without thinking.

Reactivity goes beyond anger. It stems from being hijacked by the moment and responding from emotion rather than intention. Whether it happens in a meeting, via email or in a group chat, the outcome is the same: energy gets wasted, focus gets scrambled and the situation often gets worse.

Princess Anne didn't let someone else's chaos become hers. She stayed focused. And while most of us (thankfully) won't ever have to face down a kidnapping attempt, we do face a thousand tiny ambushes every day, each one asking us to choose: reaction or response?

THE EVERYDAY HIJACK

Emergency scenarios or public heroics are thankfully rare. Most of us experience a much more mundane, everyday kind of pressure:

- The email that spikes your adrenaline
- The comment in a meeting that gets under your skin
- The text message that makes you feel like you have to explain yourself right now.

Reactivity arises in the little hijacks that most of us are walking around with all the time.

- We reply too fast.
- We snap.
- We spiral into overthinking.
- We fight fires that don't need to be fought — or that weren't even fires to begin with.

This reactivity leads us to leap without landing. Our default reflex is to respond before we've actually chosen how.

The emotions involved are not the problem because anger, frustration and fear are all human. What gets in the way is what we do with these emotions before we've even processed them. We hit send, we make the call, we say the thing and, only later, sometimes seconds later, do we think 'I probably could have handled that better.'

Reactivity is subtle:

- A tight smile and a forced 'No worries!' when you're actually furious
- Obsessively refreshing your inbox
- Apologising for things you didn't even do just to make the tension go away.

The Red Brick of Reactivity is the cost of urgency without clarity.

Learning how to pause so you can actually choose your next move, rather than have it chosen for you by your nervous system, is the red brick move — because when you start living from reaction, everything starts feeling like a crisis, and when everything feels like a crisis, nothing meaningful gets built.

This red brick isn't loud but it is substantial. If we're going to create something more deliberate — in work, in relationships, in the way we move through the world —this is one of the first red bricks that has to go. And this process begins with reclaiming the only true freedom we have.

THE FREEDOM TO CHOOSE

How often do we hear the phrase 'that triggered me' or 'I was triggered by that'? We talk about it as if it's something other people do to us, but a trigger is just that — a spark. The explosion? The reaction? That's on us.

That space between trigger and reaction? That's your power to pause.

That's it. That's the work: to find the space to *choose* how you respond and to not let every stimulus drag us by the wrist into an automatic reaction.

It sounds simple, but allowing space to choose is one of the hardest muscles to build. These pauses apply in the small, modern, daily moments we're navigating — the ones that chip away at our energy, dignity and direction:

- When someone talks over you in a meeting
- When you get the passive-aggressive email
- When someone pushes your button.

In such moments, it's better not to suppress the emotion, but instead to decide what to do with it. So next time you feel the heat rise, don't aim for perfect calm — just aim for a pause, a breath, a blink. That's where your power lives.

You can use the power in this pause to let go of the impulse to correct, control, explain or convince.

That's the heart of a now-famous poem by Cassie Phillips, an American writer and poet, called 'Just Let Them'. In essence, it's making the choice to let people believe, do and think however they like, and you simply ... let them.

It's a profound idea in a world where we're constantly nudged to explain ourselves, defend ourselves and react. But what if you didn't?

What if you choose to value your peace over being 'right'? You don't need to react — instead, you could prioritise direction over distraction and recognise that not every invitation to react is worth accepting.

YOUR AMYGDALA MADE YOU DO IT

Reactivity isn't a flaw, it's a feature — and we are wired for it.

It's your nervous system doing its job to keep you safe by responding fast. When something feels like a threat, whether it's a raised voice or a passive-aggressive email, your brain won't wait to analyse — it will launch straight into action.

There's a part of your brain called the *amygdala*. It's tiny, almond-shaped and constantly scanning for danger. Its job is to keep you alive, and it does that by acting fast. Really fast.

When the amygdala perceives a threat, it bypasses the slower, more logical parts of your brain and jumps straight into fight, flight, freeze or fawn mode:

- **Fight — control through confrontation.** When we feel threatened, our instinct may be to push back, such as by lashing out in a meeting or snapping at a colleague who challenges us. For example, you may feel cornered during a performance review and respond defensively, interrupting your manager before they finish speaking. At home, perhaps your partner gives you feedback on something small, and you immediately argue back, listing all the things *they* do wrong.

- **Flight — escape to safety.** Instead of confrontation, some of us try to get away — physically or mentally. We avoid the issue or distract ourselves with 'busy work' to keep us occupied. For example, when team conflict arises at work, you may immerse yourself in spreadsheets or emails to avoid dealing with the tension. It might show up at home after a tense family moment, when you leave the room and busy yourself cleaning the kitchen as if nothing had happened.

- **Freeze — stop and shut down.** This response is about going still. You may feel paralysed, unable to decide or act, and it's common in high-pressure environments. For example, maybe at work you're asked to present unexpectedly in a meeting and your mind goes blank — you can't think or speak. Or perhaps you get a text from a friend that feels loaded or tense, and you reread it 20 times, unsure how to respond … so you don't.

- **Fawn — people-please to stay safe.** A lesser-known but very common threat response is people-pleasing. You appease others to avoid conflict or rejection, often at your own expense. A very common workplace example is that you agree to take on another project even though your plate is full, just to keep your boss happy. Similarly, in your personal life, you might say yes to hosting a weekend event, even though you're exhausted, because you don't want to disappoint your friends.

Your amygdala doesn't ask, 'Is this a nuanced situation requiring thoughtful communication?' Instead, it yells: 'Say something! Fix it! Defend! Escape! *Now!*'

This is what psychologist Daniel Goleman has famously called an *amygdala hijack*: when your emotional brain takes over before your thinking brain even gets a chance to weigh in.

And while this reaction might have kept us alive and well in the days when threats came with sharp teeth, today the 'threats' — and our reactions — look different:

- A passive-aggressive Slack message? Snap back.

- An email copying in your boss? Formulate a pre-emptive defensive response.

- A sarcastic comment in a meeting? Give them a dirty look.

- A tone of voice that hits a nerve? Take it personally and shut down.

Your amygdala doesn't know the difference. It senses threat, so it moves you to react, and only later do you realise that your reaction probably wasn't your best moment.

Research shows that we often equate immediacy with effectiveness, perceiving faster responses as more competent, even when slower, more thoughtful actions might be wiser.

Reactivity is further fuelled by what psychologists call *negative emotional contagion:* when someone brings anxiety, anger or chaos into a room, we unconsciously mirror it. That tension jumps from one nervous system to another, unless someone chooses to stop it.

> *So, part of the work for this red brick is learning how to slow down the hijack to give the rational, grounded part of your brain enough time to catch up and say: 'Hey, this isn't a tiger — it's just a comment.'*

Let the feeling land before you launch the reply, make the call or try to fix it. Your power comes from choosing *whether* to respond, not how quickly you do it.

SPEED WITHOUT REFLECTION

Reactivity always feels productive in the moment:

- You said what needed to be said.

- You got it off your chest.

- You responded quickly and 'handled it'.

But did you? Really?

Most of the time, the costs of such snap decisions are quietly stacking up somewhere else.

- **It shows up in your energy.** It's the adrenaline crash after a heated email, the tension you carry in your jaw or shoulders, and the replay of conversations running through your mind long after they've ended.

- **It shows up in your relationships.** It's the moment a tone lands wrong and turns into a standoff because you read a message in the worst possible light … and then fired one back. And then you apologise — again — for *how* you said something instead of saying what you actually meant.

- **It shows up in your time.** Every reactive moment has a tail. You don't just spend time reacting; you spend time *recovering* from how you reacted — clarifying, smoothing over and fixing.

When you're always reacting, you're never really choosing — you're being tugged by other people's expectations, energy and urgency.

Over time, you start to lose track of what *you* want. You say yes out of habit, you agree to keep the peace, and you post, reply, engage and defend not because you're clear on what you want to say but because you're uncomfortable with not responding.

This is the Red Brick of Reactivity at work, and it is a pattern that will keep pulling you out of alignment, out of your values, out of your presence and out of your own agency if you let it.

You don't have to stop feeling things; you just have to stop letting your feelings decide everything for you.

The space between stimulus and response is where your power and agency lies. And the longer you ignore the cost of reactivity, the more expensive it gets.

THE POWER OF THE PAUSE

When Christine came to me for help, she was on edge. Every glance from a colleague, every vague email from her boss, every question asked in a meeting… she felt it all land like a punch.

- A sideways look meant they must be judging her.

- A short reply indicated that someone was annoyed.

- An innocent question in a team meeting was a veiled criticism.

She was an acknowledged expert in her field and had always been sharp, capable and respected, but she had become exhausted from interpreting every interaction as a threat. Her days became a minefield of imagined slights. Her confidence plummeted, and her performance followed suit. The story she was telling herself — *they're out to get me* — tightened its grip.

The first thing we did was simple, but powerful.

We gave her a pause button.

Whenever she felt the heat rise, her heart rate increase, her mind race or her chest tighten, she'd stop, take a breath and ask herself: 'What are three other possible explanations for what just happened?'

- Maybe her colleague was distracted, not dismissive.

- Maybe her boss was rushed, not rude.

- Maybe the question wasn't an attack, just curiosity.

At first, it felt awkward and forced, but with practice, it created just enough space to loosen the automatic reaction and let reason back in. She didn't try to turn everything into sunshine and unicorns; she simply refused to accept her first reaction as fact.

That small shift changed everything. The emotional spikes flattened, her energy returned and she became more focused, more present and more in control.

Reactivity isn't always about what's happening around us — it's about what's happening *inside* us and, sometimes, the most powerful thing we can remove is the assumption that every story our brain tells us is true.

RED FLAGS AND FAST REPLIES

Barack Obama was frequently confronted at town hall meetings by protesters shouting criticisms about healthcare or immigration reform. Cameras were always rolling, and every move he made was documented, discussed and analysed.

At any of these occasions, he could have snapped, raised his voice or made it personal.

Instead, he is well known for his more measured approach: pausing, looking the protester or heckler in the eye, and frequently working their criticism into his speech or comments.

Obama understood the Red Brick of Reactivity. He knew that if he let someone else's emotional urgency set the tone, he'd lose the room — and himself. So, he never matched their energy; instead, he redirected it.

In a thousand tiny ways, that's the same choice you get to make:

- When someone provokes you in a meeting
- When a client's email lands hard and fast
- When a colleague says something tone-deaf or triggering
- When your phone lights up with something that needs your response ... *right now.*

You don't always get to control what comes at you, but you always have a say in how you respond.

Reactivity feels powerful in the moment, but real power is measured and grounded. It knows when to speak, and when to wait.

Obama didn't win those moments because he was calm; he won them because he *chose* calm. In doing so, he didn't just hold his ground: he held the room.

The hard part about reactivity is that it rarely feels like reactivity in the moment:

- It feels like urgency.
- It feels like certainty.
- It feels like 'this needs to be handled'.

But what you're actually *feeling* is activation — and what you're actually *doing* is reacting.

And while you may not always catch it in real time, there are signs: little flags waving at you, saying, 'Hey, you're not in the driver's seat right now.'

- **You feel the sting the moment you hit send.** You fire off the message, say too much, defend too hard and, even before it lands, your brain is already drafting the apology.

- **You find yourself re-reading someone's words five times, but never once in a generous tone.** You've already decided what they meant, and it's rarely flattering.

- **You catch yourself talking to everyone else about it before you talk to the person who sent it.** Because what you really want isn't resolution, it's validation.

- **You feel the itch to reply.** You know it's not urgent, but silence makes you uncomfortable and sitting with it feels harder than reacting.

- **You notice the replay loop kicking in hours later.** You rehash the conversation, practise sharper comebacks and wonder if you were too much or not enough.

- **You feel it in your body before your brain catches up.** The tight jaw, the racing heart, the tensed shoulders ... your nervous system is getting the message before you even know why it's an issue.

- **You justify your actions by saying things like, 'I just have to get this off my chest' or 'I'm just being honest.'** Sure, you might feel these ways, but you're also being hijacked.

These signs don't make you wrong or broken, they make you human. Once you start spotting them in real time, you can start choosing differently.

Pause, breathe and buy yourself a few moments of space. That's all you need to shift from reaction to response.

REACTIVITY IS LOUD

The Red Brick of Reactivity tells you the world needs an answer from you *right now*, but this is a lie. What the world needs, and what you need, is *space*: space to breathe, to think and to remember who you are and what actually matters.

- You don't always need to raise your voice to be heard.

- You don't have to prove your point to make it.

- You are not obligated to respond to everything just because it showed up in front of you.

Reactivity can sometimes drown out presence — and the longer you stay in reaction mode, the further you drift from your own rhythm.

In one of my workshops, a participant named Charles shared something that stopped the room cold.

He said he doesn't answer his phone every time it rings, including when it's his boss calling.

You could feel the collective gasp. Ignoring a call from your boss? Letting it go to voicemail? That felt almost … rebellious.

But Charles had his reasons.

He'd noticed a pattern. Every time the boss's name flashed up on his screen, his heart rate spiked. Anxiety kicked in before he even picked up and then, mid-call, he'd stumble through his responses — rushed, reactive and not thinking clearly. Only after hanging up would he realise what he *should* have said. We've all been there, right?

Then Charles had a simple but powerful realisation: his boss had no idea whether he was in a meeting, away from his desk or in the bathroom. The urgency to pick up was imagined, so he started letting the call go to voicemail.

By doing this, he gave himself a pause: a moment to breathe, collect his thoughts and respond with composure instead of panic. He further discovered that his boss often left detailed messages, which gave Charles the advantage of gathering his thoughts before calling back.

By removing the pressure to react instantly, he reclaimed his presence and his performance.

That's Red Brick Thinking in action. Sometimes the answer isn't no, it's simply *not yet*.

The space between stimulus and response is where your whole life starts to shift.

WHERE PEACE BEGINS

Letting go of reactivity means you care enough to respond deliberately:

- You get to be the one who sets the pace.
- You get to be the one who doesn't rise to the bait.
- You get to be the one who chooses silence over spirals, curiosity over control, and direction over drama.

This red brick might be weighty, but once it's gone, you'll feel the difference in every interaction that doesn't cost you your peace.

Chapter 16
Overcommitment

In early 2023, New Zealand Prime Minister Jacinda Ardern stepped up to a podium and did something most leaders avoid at all costs.

She stopped.

With the eyes of the world on her, she announced her resignation: not amid scandal or catastrophe, but from a place of rare self-awareness. 'I no longer have enough in the tank to do the job justice,' she said. It was quiet, measured and certain.

And it boomed like a thunderclap.

Here was a woman who had led through some of the most challenging moments in modern history — a terror attack, a global pandemic and an economic recovery — saying, clearly and without apology, that she was done.

Not because she *couldn't* keep going, but because she knew she *shouldn't*.

Ardern's decision didn't come from crisis. In stepping away, she gave voice to something many leaders feel but few dare to act on: that endless resilience isn't a requirement for worthiness, and you don't have to run on empty to prove you care.

She stepped out with integrity, reframing what strength looks like in leadership. She showed that knowing when to go is just as important as knowing how to lead. That is subtraction as an act of wisdom.

Her choice made space for her, for her family, for new leadership and for a different kind of conversation: one that asks not just what we're capable of taking on, but what we're brave enough to lay down.

Ardern's departure was a masterclass in conscious subtraction. It wasn't dramatic or reactive; she'd made a clear, intentional decision to stop before she became someone she didn't recognise. It was a public, global reminder that doing less can be the most powerful move a leader makes.

We mistake availability for dedication, we confuse busyness with impact, and we carry on, often long after we've run out of capacity, because stepping back feels like we're letting others down.

It's time to challenge that story and recognise when 'I've got this' quietly turns into 'I've got too much'. The trick is to learn how to subtract *before* you break.

THE FULL-CALENDAR TRAP

Overcommitment builds quietly when the calendar fills, the list lengthens and another yes gets absorbed into the rhythm of your week without question.

There's no big moment of collapse — just a slow and permanent leak of energy. Your weekends may not be enough to replenish your strength.

It begins with opportunities — the things you're capable of, good at, even proud of — but slowly, those commitments start to layer. You forget which ones you chose freely and which ones arrived through momentum or obligation.

It evolves into that sinking feeling upon waking, when you realise your time is already spoken for before you even open your eyes. It's the heaviness of your attention fracturing across a dozen different roles, and none of them are getting the best of you. It's the slow realisation that you're doing everything except the things that might actually steady you — resting, reflecting and deciding what truly matters now.

This is how overcommitment takes hold: not with force, but with accumulation.

- The days become full but not fulfilling.
- You get through things, but nothing lands.
- You tick boxes that were never yours to begin with.

Without realising it, you're trading depth for duty, joy for productivity and space for a sense of being needed.

By the time you notice something's gone, you realise it's not just that you're low on energy, but that you've been slowly drifting away from parts of yourself you didn't notice were fading.

In 2015, when Julia came into my world, she had done what few women in Australia's financial services sector had managed to do. She'd cracked the glass ceiling.

After two decades of steady ascension — analyst, manager, director — she was named Chief Strategy Officer at one of the country's top investment firms. It was the kind of achievement that made headlines. Industry panels, awards nights and newspaper profiles made her the go-to voice on leadership, innovation and women in finance.

For a while, she wore that visibility with honour: every opportunity was a yes, every invite a nod to how far she'd come. She sat on advisory boards, mentored rising stars, took red-eye flights to international conferences and chaired taskforces that were technically outside her remit but 'too important to turn down'.

It started with small signs. She forgot things in meetings, she wasn't sleeping well, and her calendar began to feel like a list of obligations she couldn't escape. Eventually, her body stepped in with what her mind refused to acknowledge: she was burning out.

Together, we named what was happening: unintentional accumulation. She had become a collector of commitments: titles, responsibilities, speaking gigs, high-profile roles. While none of these were wrong in isolation, each one was adding a layer of weight, until they became too much.

That was the turning point.

I asked Julia to write a different kind of list — not of what to do next, but of what *not* to do anymore. As a result:

- She stepped off two boards.

- She cancelled the international speaking circuit.

- She said no to a promotion that came wrapped in prestige but promised more of the same.

It was an act of reclamation: a deliberate subtraction of the roles that looked good but no longer felt right.

Today, Julia still leads in finance, but on her terms, with clearer boundaries, deeper focus and more space to think. Her calendar is leaner, but her impact isn't.

Sometimes, the bravest thing you can do is to stop climbing and start curating.

THE PSYCHOLOGY OF TOO MUCH

Overcommitment isn't a time management issue; it's a belief system.

We say yes because it feels good: we feel helpful, capable and chosen. A request comes in, and we don't just hear the task. We hear the subtext: I trust you, I need you, you'd be great at this. In a world where being needed feels like being valued, that's a hard thing to turn down.

So, we nod, and we add.

Part of it is optimism. Psychologists call it the *planning fallacy*: the deeply human habit of underestimating how long things will take, while overestimating how much 'future us' will be able to handle. What looks like delusion is hopefulness, just slightly misapplied.

But part of it runs deeper.

Overcommitting can be a way of managing identity. When you're used to being the reliable one, the competent one, the person who gets things done, every yes feels like confirmation. It proves you're still on track, still useful and still earning your place. Saying no doesn't just risk disappointing someone; it risks shaking the story you've built about who you are.

We also carry invisible scripts:

- Be helpful.
- Be kind.
- Be generous.

These aren't bad values, but they can morph into patterns that cost us space. For many women, or anyone raised to put others first, there's a subtle social reward for self-sacrifice.

You don't just get praised for what you do. You get praised for how much you're holding.

Studies show that when people appear overloaded, they're seen as more committed, more successful and more essential. Instead of wisdom, rest reads as absence. So, we stay visible, keep moving and keep saying yes.

Overcommitment happens because we care. We say yes for the right reasons, but if we don't pause to ask what we're giving up, then we may fill our days with things that drain the energy required to enjoy them.

What wears us down isn't how big the commitments are — it's losing sight of the fact that we chose them.

WHEN EVERYTHING GETS A PIECE OF YOU

The Red Brick of Overcommitment slowly saturates our time, energy and attention until there's no space left to land.

At first, the signs are subtle.

- You start rushing through things that used to matter.

- You say yes before checking how you feel.

- You find yourself multitasking through moments that deserve your full presence.

- Your calendar becomes less of a reflection of your values, and more of a to-do list you never remember writing.

Over time, the cost rises. You become productive but disconnected, reliable but quietly resentful. You move from one task to the next without pause, unable to remember the last time you finished something and simply let yourself feel it. You're always in motion, but the meaning behind it all quickly fades.

And then there's the deeper cost. Joy becomes something you have to schedule, rest becomes something you feel you have to earn, and time alone stops feeling like a gift and starts to feel suspicious, like a warning you've missed something or let someone down.

Emotionally, overcommitment leaves you little room to feel anything fully. Gratitude feels thin, excitement feels brief, and even success starts to taste hollow when every achievement is followed by five more obligations.

Mentally, it fragments you, as every new yes dilutes your ability to focus. You're pulled in so many directions that you lose your sense of direction altogether.

And physically? Overcommitment tenses your muscles. You don't walk into your day; you brace for it.

But perhaps the greatest cost is that you slowly lose access to your own voice: the quiet knowing that says this matters, this doesn't or this can wait. That voice gets buried under deadlines, meetings, requests and well-meaning distractions, and the longer you stay overcommitted, the harder it becomes to hear yourself at all.

The true damage of saying yes to everything isn't the impact of what you take on. It's what gets crowded out and lost.

YOU'RE OVER THE LIMIT

Overcommitment doesn't always look like stress. Sometimes, it looks like achievement.

- **You notice it in the small cracks as you start resenting the very things you once enjoyed.** You keep moving — not from motivation, but from sheer momentum — saying yes even as your body quietly pleads 'not again'. You fantasise about cancelling plans because you're tired of being everywhere at once.

- **You feel it in your emotional bandwidth.** Small things irritate you, while big things overwhelm you. The space between request and reaction gets tighter; you may not be snapping, but you're holding your breath a lot.

- **You catch it in the way your mind scatters.** Tasks get done but don't feel satisfying, conversations blur together, and you reread the same paragraph twice and still don't absorb it.

- **You sense it in your body before your mind admits it.** Sleep isn't refreshing and breaks don't relax you. Your shoulders ache, your jaw tightens and you describe your days as hectic, nonstop or 'Fine, I guess.'

And you might recognise it in the deepest way. You don't feel like you're failing; you just don't feel like yourself anymore.

When that becomes the baseline, it's time to ask: 'What am I giving my time, energy and care to that no longer deserves it?'

THE JOY OF SPACE IS UNDERRATED

In a world addicted to busyness, we've been conditioned to treat empty space like a problem that needs solving.

- Free time? Fill it.

- Downtime? Optimise it.

- Calendar gap? Plug it with another meeting, another call, another commitment.

But presence doesn't live in packed schedules — it lives in the space between things.

Kate Christie, global bestselling author of *The Life List: Master Every Moment and Live an Audacious Life*, believes the key to a meaningful life isn't finding more time, it's using the time you already have with intention.

When I spoke with her about the idea of Red Brick Thinking, she agreed that overcommitment gets in the way of us living our best lives.

'Too often we hold back on living our best life. We wait for "later" or for the right moment or to be less busy. This is an active choice — so make a better choice: choose to free up your time to invest it in what you value most,' Christie said. 'Instead of adding to your to-do list, work out what you can reject or subtract from it. Give every activity a score out of 10: how much do I love this activity, is it something I have chosen for myself or has it been chosen for me? If a task gets less than an 8 then this is an activity you can potentially reject from your life. Because the future is not certain. Your health, energy and opportunity are not guaranteed. The risk of waiting to start living is that you may never get to do the things that matter most to you.'

Kate's message is clear. Don't wait for the perfect time; live now.

A meaningful life isn't managed — it's chosen.

THE JOY OF FEWER THINGS, DONE FULLY

There's something quietly profound about being *all in*: not half-committed, not toggling between distractions, not squeezing in something meaningful between pings, notifications or another round of digital multitasking, but being *fully there*, fully engaged and fully human.

I first heard Peter Cook — mentor, entrepreneur and bestselling author — talk about this idea in 2016: that it's much harder to be 99 per cent committed to something than 100 per cent. That last 1 per cent is where resistance lives — where doubt creeps in and distractions multiply. But when you commit fully, when you choose clearly and completely what gets your attention, you unlock a kind of simplicity that feels almost sacred.

That kind of focus happens when you're brave enough to decide what *doesn't* deserve your attention.

In Sweden, there's a cultural principle known as *lagom*. It means not too much, not too little — just enough.

- It's the antithesis of hustle culture.

- It doesn't demand maximisation.

- It invites presence.

- It's the art of knowing when to stop, when to say no and when to let something be — not because you're lazy, but because you're wise enough to know when enough is enough.

Lagom doesn't show up in pitch decks, and it may not be a trending hashtag, but it's the quiet engine behind lives that feel whole, not hurried. *Lagom* is about sufficiency, and in a world that constantly tells you to want more, *enough* becomes revolutionary.

You don't need to do everything to live a rich life. You just need to do the right things, deeply.

That's the essence of Red Brick Thinking:

- Choosing depth over breadth
- Choosing presence over productivity
- Choosing to subtract so that what matters most can be heard and felt.

Most of us aren't overwhelmed because we have too little time; we're overwhelmed because we're spread too thin across too many commitments and too many priorities. We have too many tabs open, mentally and literally.

But when you decide, with intention, to do fewer things fully? That's where the richness lives.

And that's the life you remember.

DESIGNING YOUR OWN RED BRICK LIFE

Designing a life that matters doesn't require you to abandon society, move to the mountains or quit your job in a grand, cinematic gesture. It's rarely that dramatic. More often, it's quieter and far more daring.

It looks like choosing. Not once, but repeatedly.

It looks like small, deliberate decisions made day after day:

- What am I no longer available for?
- What dream no longer belongs to me?
- Where have I confused being capable with being called?

These are not questions you answer once and move on from. They're questions that become part of your rhythm — your personal audit for a life of intention. Because the reality is that it's dangerously easy to build a life filled with things that no longer belong to you: expectations you inherited, roles you never questioned and dreams that were never truly yours.

Red Brick Thinking doesn't ask you to reject ambition or success, cut back to prove a point or live smaller for the sake of virtue.

Red Brick Thinking asks you to subtract what doesn't serve you in order to make space for what does.

You don't need to do more to matter, or to prove your worth through how busy or burned out you are. What you need is the space to listen to yourself without the clamour of constant commitments, so you can act with intention instead of from impulse, and do fewer things but give them the full weight of your presence.

At the end of your life, you won't wish you'd done more — you'll wish you'd felt more and been more present, honest and connected. You'll wish you'd made space for what really mattered.

That's the red brick way: subtraction as a strategy, not a sacrifice.

You don't want to shrink your life. You want to sharpen it.

Chapter 17

Obligation

In March 2022, the tennis world stopped mid-rally.

Ash Barty, then world number one and fresh off her Australian Open victory, announced — without fanfare, without scandal and without regret — that she was retiring. At 25 years old and at the absolute peak of her career. Healthy, dominant and unmatched.

The news broke like a glitch in the matrix.

Commentators scrambled for reasons. Was she injured? Pregnant? Burned out? Was it a publicity stunt?

'I don't have the physical drive, the emotional want and everything it takes to challenge yourself at the very top of the level anymore,' she told close friend Casey Dellacqua in an Instagram video.

The sports media didn't quite know what to do with that.

Barty wasn't walking away in disgrace. She had just become the first Australian woman in 44 years to win the Australian Open, achieving her childhood dream in front of a roaring home crowd. This was *supposed* to be her victory lap, not her exit.

But Barty has never been interested in doing what she was 'supposed' to do, and this wasn't the first time.

Back in 2014, she had already stunned fans by quitting tennis at age 18. At the time, she was one of the most promising young players in the world, but instead of pushing through, she took a break and signed with the Brisbane Heat as a professional cricketer. Not just a publicity guest, she played, competed and held her own in a completely different sport, in front of completely different crowds. When asked why, she simply said, 'In short, I think I needed just to find myself. I felt like I got twisted and maybe a little bit lost along the way in the first part of my career.'

Eventually, she found her way back to tennis on her own terms.

What followed was one of the most remarkable comebacks in modern sport. Between 2016 and 2022, Barty went from outsider to icon. She won Wimbledon, the French Open and the Australian Open. She held the world number one ranking for 114 consecutive weeks. She became the face of grace under pressure, admired not just for her wins but for how she *carried* them: without drama, without ego.

And then, just like before, she walked away.

The media didn't know where to file her. There was no hunger for legacy or clinging to relevance. No trying to turn her name into a brand. She simply said she was ready for the next chapter of her life — a quieter one, away from the circuit, where success didn't need to be televised.

To many, it looked like a waste: a betrayal of potential and a missed opportunity to 'build her empire'.

But to those paying closer attention, it looked like something else entirely.

Ash Barty never let obligation dictate the shape of her life. She left when she needed to leave and returned when she was ready, and then she exited again — not with apologies, but with peace. No matter how loud the world got, she kept listening to herself.

That's the quiet power of Red Brick Thinking: the courage to step away from what no longer feels true, even when the world expects you to keep climbing.

You walk away if you want to because you're free to do so.

THE WEIGHT OF INHERITED EXPECTATIONS

The Red Brick of Obligation is the quiet load we carry not because we want to, but because we feel we should.

Obligation comes in many forms:

- The project you didn't initiate but feel responsible for
- The family tradition you've long outgrown but still uphold
- The version of success that once excited you but now feels like a job description you forgot to quit.

Obligation is shifty because it speaks the language of duty and maturity. It tells you that showing up, even when it drains you, is noble. It suggests that quitting is weakness, and that walking away means you're ungrateful — so we keep performing the life we once said yes to, even after it has stopped fitting.

Sometimes, we keep going because we're good at it, we think we owe someone or we've just been doing it for so long that we don't remember how to stop.

What once was aligned has become outdated — and the longer we ignore that, the heavier it gets.

Obligation never starts as a trap. It starts as a promise and, over time, that promise can become a performance — and the role we're playing isn't always the one we chose.

INVISIBLE CONTRACTS

Obligation has deep roots in our psychology.

From early childhood, we're wired for connection and approval. Psychologist Carl Rogers wrote that when acceptance is conditional — based on behaviour, performance or helpfulness — we start to internalise the idea that love must be earned. We begin to accept that being 'good' means doing what's expected, even at the cost of authenticity.

Obligation begins in how we learn to belong.

Over time, this conditioning morphs into what researchers call *role entrapment*: when we become locked into identities and responsibilities not because they energise us, but because they've become how we're known, trusted or needed.

This is particularly strong in high-functioning, highly capable people. Studies in occupational psychology show that those seen as reliable often become default holders of responsibility, even without formal assignment. The reward for being dependable is that you are given more to carry.

Social pressure adds another layer. Sociologist Erving Goffman described our public lives as a series of performances. Once you've been applauded for a role, be it the reliable colleague, the tireless parent or the overachiever, it's harder to set it down. You're not just disappointing others; you're disrupting the narrative.

And then there's the guilt economy. Behavioural science research shows that guilt is one of the most potent emotional drivers of compliance. Women in particular, and people raised in collectivist cultures, are more likely to associate saying no with selfishness — not because they lack boundaries, but because they've been taught to measure worth in terms of self-sacrifice.

Combine all this, and obligation becomes sticky.

It feels like responsibility and looks like consistency. Even when it quietly erodes joy, we rationalise it as part of being a grown-up.

But what looks like responsibility is often just inertia in disguise.

We keep going because it's familiar. We are tied to our obligations because someone else once expected it of us, and we haven't yet given ourselves permission to stop.

At first, obligation feels like being a good person: you do the right thing, you show up and you follow through. But slowly, subtly, it starts to chip away at your energy. Not in big, dramatic cracks but in quiet erosion.

- You stop asking what you want, because you're so busy delivering what others need.

- Your days become filled with tasks that feel disconnected from meaning.

- You feel stretched thin but can't point to any one thing to put down.

Everything you do feels justifiable, reasonable and expected. But this is the real cost of obligation — a life that looks full but feels hollow.

A life that belongs to everyone but you.

My friend and client, Stuart, ran a third-generation family farm in regional Victoria. He was the kind of person everyone relied on: the one who showed up early, stayed late, remembered birthdays, fixed fences and never said no when someone asked for help.

To most, he looked like the model of generosity — salt of the earth, reliable and steady.

But inside, Stuart was tired. Deeply tired.

It wasn't the work, because he loved the land. It was the constant sense of *should* that wore him down.

- He *should* help out at the footy club.

- He *should* keep the family traditions going.

- He *should* say yes when the neighbour asks to borrow his ute … again.

Somewhere along the way, his life had stopped feeling like his own and started to feel like a checklist of inherited obligations.

When we started working together, Stuart didn't talk about burnout. He talked about guilt: the guilt of saying no, the fear of letting people down, the quiet resentment that followed every yes he didn't want to give.

So, we started small.

We talked about choosing, not defaulting. About giving out of *willingness* rather than *weariness*. I asked him to try one thing: next time someone makes a request, pause, just for a beat, and ask himself, 'If I say yes to this, what am I saying no to?'

He tried it once. Then again. And slowly, things began to shift.

Stuart didn't become selfish; he became selective. He started saying no without over-explaining, he stopped attending things out of obligation, and he started showing up where it mattered most to him. The footy club didn't fall apart, his family still called and, for the first time in years, Stuart started to feel like he had space in his own life again.

Obligation had made him dependable, but intention made him deliberate.

Red Brick Thinking asks you to notice the contracts you've signed without realising — to pause and ask, 'Who did I agree to be and do I still want to be that?'

Because you can renegotiate the role and rewrite the terms. You can stop showing up as the version of you that people expect and start showing up as the version that feels true.

You don't owe anyone a lifetime subscription to a role you've outgrown.

TETHERED BY EXPECTATIONS

Obligation feels responsible, adult, even noble, but there are signals, small and persistent, that you're being controlled by commitments that no longer reflect who you are or what you want.

- **Your calendar feels full, but your heart doesn't.**
  You're attending, responding, delivering, but little of
  it feels energising. You're showing up out of habit, not
  hunger — and when someone cancels a meeting, your first
  feeling is relief.

- **You feel guilty even *thinking* about saying no.** You've
  tied your value to being dependable, so you say yes quickly,
  instinctively, then regret it quietly later. The resentment
  builds, but so does the guilt.

- **You can't remember the last time you chose something
  just for yourself.** Your time is accounted for; your energy
  is pre-allocated. Even rest feels strategic or squeezed into
  the margins. You've forgotten what it means to choose
  without justification.

- **You're succeeding at things you no longer care about.**
  The external markers are there — accomplishments,
  praise, progress — but they land flat. You wonder why you

don't feel prouder or more alive, yet you still keep ticking the boxes.

- **You feel tension when someone asks, 'What do you want?'** You're not sure what the answer is, or perhaps the answer feels inconvenient in relation to everything you've built. You've lost touch with your own desires beneath the layers of other people's expectations.

These signs aren't proof that you're failing. They're proof that you're human and that, somewhere along the way, a script took over. It's time to reread that script with fresh eyes.

THE SOCIAL SCRIPT PROBLEM

It's the unwritten storyline we're all handed at birth: go to school, work hard, get a good job, buy a house, have a family, climb the ladder, retire and then, finally, rest.

The specifics vary, but the shape stays the same: a linear trajectory towards 'having it all' and, if we're lucky, we'll tick all the boxes with a smile.

- We rarely talk about wanting less.
- We never leave 'good jobs'.
- We certainly don't walk away from stability, unless we have a better plan, all fully mapped out.

The script doesn't reward exploration; it rewards certainty.

But here's the thing about scripts: most of us never question who wrote them. We just start reading the lines.

The social script is not always oppressive, but it can be irresistible. Often, it's comfortable, logical and admired. However, Red Brick Thinking asks:

- Whose definition of success are you living?

- What milestones are you chasing out of habit, not hunger?

- What have you told yourself it's too late to change?

You don't have to abandon your whole life, but you do get to question the role you're playing.

That's the trap of the social script:

- It rewards compliance.

- It validates sameness.

- It turns real lives into checklists.

And if you dare to opt out, it calls you ungrateful, unambitious or lost.

You can leave the script, improvise or rewrite it because the best stories are rarely the ones we were handed — they're the ones we were brave enough to reimagine.

CAPABILITY ≠ CALLING

We don't get trapped by failure; we get trapped by *excellence*. It's one of the hardest lessons to learn, especially for those who are deeply competent, deeply trusted and deeply tired.

We become so good at something, so reliable, so praised for our ability, that we begin to confuse it with purpose. We start to believe that just because we *can*, we *should*—and the more capable we are, the more difficult it becomes to walk away.

How do you step back from something you're brilliant at—that others rely on you for, and that's come to define how the world sees you?

Red Brick Thinking reminds us that just because you're good at something, it doesn't mean it's yours to carry forever.

I've spent decades writing about what makes for good training and delivering train-the-trainer programs. I'm good enough at it that the requests still come regularly and, for a long time, I said yes almost automatically because being capable made me feel like I should.

But capability is not the same as calling.

Just because I *can* run those programs, it doesn't mean I always *should*. These days, if I take them on, it's because I choose to: not out of obligation, not because it's expected, but because sometimes it feels good to do something familiar and comfortable, on my terms.

It took me a long time to realise that skill isn't the same as purpose. Being good at something doesn't mean you owe it your energy forever. Sometimes, the most powerful thing you can do with your capabilities is to choose when and how you use them—not just prove that you can.

Equally, just because you said something once, it doesn't mean you have to believe it forever.

A colleague and I were having one of those between-meetings chats—the kind that starts with small talk and ends up somewhere far more interesting. She was telling me about a tricky stakeholder situation she'd finally found a way through. Nothing dramatic, just one of those slow-burn work relationships where everything feels harder than it should. Misread emails, awkward meetings and constant second-guessing had left her wondering what was going on.

'I thought she didn't like me,' my colleague admitted. 'Honestly, two weeks ago I was convinced she was trying to edge me out of the project.'

Then she paused, smiled and shook her head. 'Now I realise … she was just overwhelmed and probably thinking the same thing about me.'

We laughed and I said one of my favourite lines: 'I can't believe how stupid I was two weeks ago.'

It landed as intended — not as a judgement but as a relief.

Because growth isn't always loud. Sometimes it happens in the quiet moment when you realise the story you were telling yourself no longer fits. The certainty you clung to has dissolved and you're left with a little more insight, and a lot more compassion.

'I can't believe how stupid I was two weeks ago' isn't about regret. It's proof that we're learning and that we're flexible enough to change our minds. If we're lucky, we'll keep looking back and cringing just enough to know we're getting better.

Your calling can change, your energy can shift, and your life is allowed to reflect that.

So many of us stay in roles, formal and informal, because we don't want to let people down. We don't know what else we'd be without the label, and we've been told that quitting is failure.

But maybe the real failure is staying in a story that no longer fits, just because we know how to play the part.

Capability is a gift, but a calling is your compass.

IT'S OKAY TO WALK AWAY

The tension between staying for the sake of others or leaving for the sake of yourself is especially present in cultures shaped by quiet self-restraint.

In the Nordic countries, there's a cultural code called *jante*, the law of modesty. Originating in fiction, it has become mainstream. Unspoken, but deeply felt, it teaches people not to stand out:

- Don't be too proud.
- Don't think you're special.
- Don't make others uncomfortable with your ambition.

It creates a powerful social cohesion, but it can also lead to deep self-suppression.

We have our very own version of this in Australia called *tall poppy syndrome*. You'd better believe that if you stick your head up (like a poppy) there will be someone waiting to cut you down.

When you're taught to value harmony above all else, you learn to silence your inner disruption.

- You stay in jobs you've outgrown.

- You keep leading projects you no longer believe in.

- You show up in spaces where your energy is no longer welcome because leaving might make someone else uncomfortable.

Red Brick Thinking reframes walking away not as giving up, but as reclaiming your time, your energy and your right to evolve.

Permission to walk away is permission to update the contract: not just with your employer, your community or your family, but with yourself.

Walking away is a conscious return to what matters: a return to who you are, beneath the obligations. It doesn't require a crisis — it just requires *a deep breath* before you say:

- 'This no longer fits.'

- 'I am not the same person who said yes to this.'

- 'I can respect where this brought me and still choose a different way forward.'

The opposite of obligation isn't selfishness — it's alignment. By saying no to what isn't yours anymore, you can make space to say yes to what is.

While the world rewards endurance, your soul rewards *alignment*.

Chapter 18

Relationships

Jelena Dokic is another of Australia's brightest tennis stars. At her peak, she reached world number four. For much of her tennis journey, while carrying a nation's hopes on her shoulders, her father was right beside her.

From the outside, they looked like a tight-knit team: a demanding but dedicated coach, pushing his daughter to greatness. But behind the scenes, Jelena was living through something very different.

In interviews and in her memoir, *Unbreakable*, she describes the physical abuse, the emotional manipulation, the relentless pressure and the fear. Her success had become something she survived rather than something she could enjoy.

And still, she stayed.

She knew what was happening was wrong, but she was also taught that family is sacred: that you don't cut off your blood because loyalty matters more than safety. And when the world sees someone as a 'difficult father' or a 'strict coach' instead of what he really is, it's easier to keep quiet than to be disbelieved.

But eventually, Jelena made a different choice. In 2014, she cut ties with her father. She walked away not just from a person, but from a story she'd been told she had to keep living.

Since then, she's found her voice as a commentator, an advocate and as someone willing to tell the truth, even when it's hard — and in doing so, she's helped others.

Not all relationship red bricks look toxic on the outside. Some look like tradition, some look like love and some look like the people who raised you.

But if they cost you your peace, your self-worth or your future, they don't belong in the next version of your life.

We often talk about endings as failures:

- Failed businesses
- Failed friendships
- Failed marriages
- Failed teams.

We're wired to hold on, especially when it comes to people. We're taught that commitment is a virtue, loyalty is noble and walking away makes us cold or ungrateful. So, we cling, we accommodate, we compromise and we keep certain people in our lives, in our inboxes or on our calendars long after the connection has expired.

Sometimes we hold on not because we still want the relationship, but because we're scared of what it means to let it go.

But here's the thing:

- Not every relationship was meant to last forever.

- Not every dynamic is meant to evolve.

- Not everyone in your life is meant to go the distance.

Letting go of a relationship isn't weak. In fact, sometimes it's the bravest, most generous thing you can do for them and for yourself.

You don't have to wait until the relationship becomes toxic. You don't have to justify it with drama, and you don't even need a 'good reason'. You just need honesty and the willingness to say, 'This doesn't belong in the next version of my life.'

This chapter is about the people:

- Who drain more than they give

- Who you've outgrown

- Who take up time, energy and attention that could be better spent elsewhere.

They might not be bad people, but that doesn't mean they belong in your close orbit.

TETHERED BY HABIT, NOT HEART

This red brick is subtle: a feeling of friction you can't quite explain, an audible exhale after a phone call, a drained sense of self after a coffee catch-up, or a message you don't want to answer but feel you should.

This is the Red Brick of Relationships — the ones that cost more than they give.

This red brick is not about the relationships that stretch you or challenge you in good ways, but the ones that consistently pull your energy down rather than lift it up:

- A long-time friend you've simply outgrown
- A colleague you're constantly managing emotionally
- A client who chips away at your boundaries
- A mentor whose advice no longer lands
- A group chat you stay in out of habit, not joy
- A social media connection who grates against your values.

What unites them isn't who they are, it's how they make us feel — drained, depleted and diminished.

We often stay because we feel bad, we don't want to be rude or it used to be good. We also worry what people will think if we step away. So, we convince ourselves it's fine, manageable and not that bad, until the weight of these small, ongoing misalignments starts to show up everywhere in our time, our energy, our attention and our sense of self.

WHEN HISTORY BECOMES A TRAP

We hold on for a thousand quiet reasons, none of which feel like permission to walk away.

- Because we've known them forever
- Because they were there for us once

- Because we don't want to be the bad person

- Because they *need* us

- Because we're scared of what happens when they're not in our lives anymore.

We tell ourselves that leaving would be simple if the signs were clear or if something exploded — maybe if they betrayed us, or it all fell apart.

But that's not how most relationships end. They fade, calcify and become something different, quieter, duller, heavier — and yet still, we stay.

Maybe it's the relationship version of the sunk-cost fallacy: the idea that once we've poured time, energy or love into someone, we feel compelled to stick it out, even when we know better or we've already outgrown the shape of the connection.

We think: 'But I've already given so much.' It's as if that effort should mean something — as if walking away now would waste everything we've invested. Staying longer doesn't redeem the past; it just costs you more of the present.

We're wired to feel the pain of loss more deeply than the pleasure of gain. Psychologists call it *loss aversion*, and it shapes more of our decisions than we realise. Even when a relationship is weighing us down, we fear what we'll lose more than we feel hope for what we might gain. The routine, the shared history and the comfort of the familiar all become reasons to endure.

Add to that the quiet grip of attachment patterns, and relationships can become an agonising red brick to manage. If you've ever stayed longer than you should have because you didn't want to hurt someone, you didn't want to be alone or you didn't know who you'd be without the role you'd been playing in their life, that's not personal defeat — that's your nervous system doing its job. It's trying to keep you safe, even when safety means staying small.

And underneath it all is the voice in your head that convinces you, 'It's not that bad,' 'Maybe you're just being dramatic' or 'You've been through worse.'

That voice has a name too: *cognitive dissonance*, the internal tension we feel when our actions don't match our beliefs. So, instead of making a change, we bend our thinking, we downplay the pain and we justify the status quo. Change would mean confronting the fact that we've stayed too long, that we've known for a while and that we've been afraid.

We don't just stay for them; we stay for the version of us that promised this would work.

If we don't leave, we accommodate, shrinking ourselves into the shape that still fits the relationship, even if it no longer fits *us*.

At some point, if you're brave enough to listen, you'll hear the truth rise up from underneath the rationalisations:

- You're not a bad person for wanting space.

- You're not selfish for needing something else.

- You're not broken because something that once felt right … doesn't anymore.

You're just ready.

KEEPING THE PEACE

We tell ourselves that holding on keeps us safe, keeps things calm, keeps the peace, but the real cost is harder to see. It's the time you'll never get back, the energy you keep spending on something that no longer feeds you and the mental space that could have been used for something better — something more alive.

Most of all, it's the grounded part of yourself that you keep suppressing — the part of you that knows better but so often gets sidelined to avoid rocking the boat.

When you stay in relationships that are misaligned, draining or simply outdated, you're not just keeping the peace — you're delaying your own progress. You find yourself editing what you say, managing their moods or overthinking every message before you send it. You replay conversations that didn't sit right, but you brush the feeling aside. You go to the coffee catch-up because it would be rude not to. You stay in the group chat because leaving would be awkward. You say yes when every part of you is quietly whispering no.

This is the real weight of staying too long: not the big blowups, not the drama, but the slow erosion of your time, your energy and your truth.

Over time, it builds up and you lose the ability to hear your own voice:

* You can't do meaningful work when your emotional inbox is full.

- You can't access creativity when you're in constant repair mode.

- You can't be fully present when part of your mind is always scanning for friction.

This is the tax of people-pleasing, politeness and staying too long.

We often feel drained or rushed because we've given our time and energy to places when there is little return.

Removing this red brick isn't just about walking away from someone. It's about walking back towards yourself.

YOU'RE THERE, BUT YOU'RE NOT REALLY YOU

Sometimes we don't even realise we're holding on too tightly, until we start to feel the strain.

The signs aren't always loud. Often, they're subtle, small but consistent.

- **You feel heavy after spending time with them.** It's like a low-grade emotional hangover that leaves you tired, flat or vaguely irritated.

- **You rehearse conversations in your head.** You're editing yourself constantly, considering what you should say, what you can't say and how to avoid upsetting them.

- **You dread the catch-up but do it anyway.** You're acting out of guilt, habit or obligation. You spend the whole drive there talking yourself into it, and the whole drive home wondering why you went.

- **You feel like you're managing them.** You're not relating to them; you're caretaking their emotions, their needs and their drama.

- **You feel smaller when you're with them.** You're less bold, less open, less *you*. You shrink a little just to keep the peace.

- **You're always the one making the effort.** You make the calls, send the texts, initiate the conversations. If you stopped trying, the connection would probably fade on its own.

- **You justify their behaviour to yourself and others.** You spend more time explaining the relationship than enjoying it: 'They're just going through a lot.' 'They mean well.' 'That's just how they are.'

Any one of these things, on occasion, is human, but it's when they become a pattern that it's a sign something's not working.

There's a point in every relationship — personal, professional or creative — when you have to stop and ask: 'Is this still working for me?'

In 2018, Taylor Swift hit that point.

After a 12-year run with Big Machine Records, the label that helped launch her career, she made the decision to walk away.

Taylor had one core desire: to own her work.

She'd spent years building her catalogue, one song at a time. But despite her success, the masters of her first six albums remained in the hands of the label, so when the chance to re-sign came up, she asked for ownership. But ownership wasn't on offer, so she walked.

On the surface, it looked like a bold career move; underneath, it was a deeply human one. She chose to leave a long-standing, successful relationship because their values no longer aligned.

Then came the tipping point.

In 2019, Big Machine was sold to Scooter Braun's Ithaca Holdings, along with the masters of Swift's early work. Taylor didn't mince words. She called the acquisition 'my worst-case scenario'. On the surface it looked like a business deal, but to her it was a reminder of what she no longer had control over — and why walking away had been the right call.

Rather than fight to get her old music back, she did something that surprised the whole music industry: she started re-recording all of it from scratch. Album by album, track by track, she reclaimed her work on her terms. 'Taylor's Versions' went beyond branding. Releasing them was a statement: a manifesto of ownership, integrity and agency.

You don't have to be a global superstar to feel the same thing in your own world. Whether it's a business partner, a friend or a client, there are relationships we stay in long after they stop making sense. We tell ourselves we're lucky to be here. We settle and we adapt, until something happens that shows us it's time to move on.

Swift didn't wait for permission; she made the call, from a place of conviction rather than bitterness.

And sometimes, that's all it takes.

RELEASING WITHOUT RESENTMENT

The Red Brick of Relationships requires us to be honest with ourselves. Once you see the signs, it becomes harder to unsee them — and from there, you get to choose what happens next.

Letting go of a relationship is the clearest sign that you're listening to yourself again: that you've stopped outsourcing your energy and you're building a life on purpose, not out of politeness.

This red brick, whatever it looks like for you, doesn't need to be thrown. It just needs to be set down gently — and when you do, you'll feel it:

- A little more space
- A little more ease
- A little more you.

You don't need to hate someone to decide they no longer belong in your life. You just need to love your time, your peace and your future a little more.

PART 5
THE RED BRICK REVOLUTION

red brick

/ˈrɛd brɪk/

noun

Definition:

A mindset or problem-solving approach that prioritises removal over addition.

Usage:

'Red Brick Thinking saved our strategy day. We scrapped half the agenda and focused on the conversations that actually mattered.'

'She brings a Red Brick Thinking lens to every project, always asking what we can stop doing.'

'He removed the Red Brick of Noise, and suddenly we all had more breathing room in our schedules.'

verb (used with object)

Definition:

To intentionally remove or eliminate something that is unnecessary, outdated or obstructive in order to restore clarity, efficiency or focus.

Usage:

'Let's red brick this meeting agenda. It's cluttered with items we don't need.'

'She red bricked half her to-do list and finally had time to think.'

'He red bricked his entire inbox by declaring email bankruptcy and starting fresh at zero.'

We've spent the bulk of this book looking inward at the habits, defaults and assumptions that keep us stuck in cycles of addition. We've peeled back the layers of busyness, perfectionism, obligation and excess. We've asked hard questions and removed what doesn't serve us.

Now, the real opportunity begins.

Because once you start thinking this way, you can't unsee it. The unnecessary stands out, the clutter becomes obvious and the weight of 'more' feels heavier than ever.

This is the moment Red Brick Thinking stops being personal and starts becoming powerful: when it stops being a concept or a noun and starts being an action. A verb.

This is the Red Brick Revolution.

It's not a noisy, banner-waving kind of revolution; it's a quiet, clear-eyed way of thinking that reshapes how we show up in our teams, our organisations and our lives.

It's a revolution of subtraction and simplicity — of making space.

This isn't just about you anymore.

This is about the ripple effect that begins when one person chooses to red brick their world and then invites others to do the same.

Chapter 19

Just red brick it

Red Brick Thinking isn't just an idea to admire: it's a skill to practise, a habit to develop and a tool to carry with you every day. The more you use it, the more you notice what needs to go. You begin to see friction for what it is — a red brick waiting to be pulled.

And here's the best part: this isn't about waiting for the perfect moment, or getting sign-off, or following a 10-step program. Red Brick Thinking is fast and freeing.

So, the questions become:

- Where can you apply it right now?

- What's unbalanced, bloated or overworked in your world?

- What could shift if you stopped trying to add and chose to remove instead?

Let's stop *thinking* about red bricks and start *removing* them.

RED BRICK THINKING AS A DAILY PRACTICE

Stop tolerating what drains you. Interrupt the autopilot and start asking, clearly and consistently, 'Why are we still doing this?'

This is not the time for waiting or overthinking. It's the time for action: not grand gestures or full reinventions, just small, deliberate removals. That's where real insight begins.

- Cancel a meeting no one needs? That's a small 'r' red brick.

- Unsubscribe from the newsletter you never read? Small 'r'.

- Say no to a request that doesn't align? Still small 'r' but with a bigger ripple.

- Delete a slide that confuses more than it clarifies? Absolutely Red Brick Thinking.

Each of these small 'r' red bricks are quick, quiet and powerful in repetition. They build the muscle, sharpen your edge and, when done consistently, they prepare you for the bigger work because, eventually, you'll face a red brick with a big 'R':

- The role you've outgrown

- The strategy that no longer drives

- The way of working that's burning you out.

These big 'R' red bricks are the ones that create the most space when removed. You'll only have the courage to face them if you've built the habit of subtracting the small things first.

This is Red Brick Thinking as a daily discipline. You stop adding by default and start removing by design.

Once you start seeing through that lens, you don't just change how you work.

You change how you see.

THE RED BRICK LOOP

Red Brick Thinking works best when it becomes second nature, like a reflex or a rhythm.

Here's a process you can run — anytime, anywhere — to stay in the practice:

1. **Spot it.** Notice the friction, the eyeroll, the energy drop — that moment you think, 'Why are we doing this again?' That's the red brick revealing itself.

2. **Question it.** Ask: 'Does this still deliver the outcome? Or is it just habit? If it disappeared, would anyone miss it? Would anything break, or would things actually flow better?'

3. **Remove it.** Don't tweak or shift it sideways, just pull it. Say no. Cancel it. Delete it. Unplug it. You'll be amazed how often nothing bad happens, and how much space opens up.

4. **Feel it.** Notice what changes. Clarity? Relief? Time? Headspace? Red Brick Thinking creates feedback, so tune into it, learn from it and use it to spot the next red brick.

5. **Talk about it.** Share your experience with others and encourage them to apply Red Brick Thinking in their world and feel the difference.

You can run this loop in less than five minutes flat. Seconds even.

Over time, you won't even think about the steps — you'll just feel when something's off and know it's time to act. You'll become the kind of person who clears the path instead of adding to the clutter.

You won't become a minimalist; instead, you'll become a *removalist* — someone who makes progress by pulling back.

EVERYWHERE YOU LOOK

Red Brick Thinking doesn't need a big whiteboard session or a strategy meeting off-site.

It happens in moments: in small choices and tiny, often invisible removals that free up time, energy and attention.

Let's bring it to life in three spaces where red bricks love to hide: your personal life, your workplace and your leadership roles.

PERSONAL: THE NOISE YOU'VE NORMALISED

Your day is full of habits and inputs that quietly pile up. Left unchecked, they become a kind of invisible load, and you don't even notice the drag until you start removing it.

Red Brick Thinking in your personal life looks like:

- Deleting unused apps that clutter your phone (and mind)
- Removing tasks from your to-do list that you're never going to do and don't need to do
- Saying no to a social catch-up that drains instead of fuels
- Dropping the self-talk that says, 'I should be doing more.'

One of my clients, Rebecca, realised her morning routine had been hijacked by doom-scrolling and mental load. Instead of adding a new mindfulness app, she red bricked the habit of checking her phone first thing. Within a week, she had more space in her head and a sense of calm she hadn't felt in years. No new tool required: just one thing removed.

WORKPLACE: THE THINGS THAT DON'T DESERVE YOUR TIME

Meetings. Reports. Processes. Requests. Tools that promise efficiency but deliver overwhelm. Workplaces are full of red bricks dressed up to seem essential.

Red Brick Thinking at work might mean:

- Cancelling a recurring meeting that no longer has a purpose
- Ending the use of a reporting template that no one reads
- Consolidating five shared drives into one
- Saying, 'We don't need a new tool. We need fewer tools.'

Joseph, a LinkedIn follower, sent me a DM (direct message) to share how he once took one look at his team's weekly reporting process and asked, 'Who's actually reading these?' When no one gave a clear answer, he scrapped the 12-slide PowerPoint updates and replaced them with three bullet points in a shared doc. No one missed the slides and his whole team got an hour of their lives back.

That's some wicked Red Brick Thinking right there.

LEADERSHIP: SUBTRACT TO CLEAR THE PATH

At the leadership level, Red Brick Thinking isn't just tactical; it's cultural. It's about removing complexity so others can thrive.

Red Brick Thinking in leadership roles might look like:

- Scrapping outdated KPIs that no longer reflect the direction of the team

- Cutting the 40-slide strategy deck down to five slides that actually say something

- Eliminating the need for approval loops that slow decisions to a crawl

- Saying, 'That priority doesn't belong here anymore.'

Johanna, a CEO and early adopter of Red Brick Thinking, started every quarter by asking her exec team, 'What are we not doing this quarter?' She'd made Red Brick Thinking part of the planning: not as a nice-to-have, but as a leadership responsibility.

BUT WHAT IF ...?

Every red brick you spot comes with a quiet little voice in the back of your mind that says:

- 'But we've always done it this way.'

- 'What if we need it later?'

- 'It might upset someone.'

This is resistance talking. Not reason, strategy or foresight: just fear, dressed up as logic.

We tell ourselves we're being careful, respectful and strategic but, often, we're just avoiding the discomfort of change, of letting go, of being the one who questions the thing no one else will touch.

Let's break these down.

'BUT WE'VE ALWAYS DONE IT THIS WAY.'

So what? Some of the most inefficient processes in workplaces today are there simply because no one wanted to be the one to stop them.

Tradition doesn't equal effectiveness, and longevity doesn't equal value.

My client Christina inherited a monthly business review meeting with 12 people and a 48-slides-long deck. When she asked, 'Why do we do it this way?' the answer was literally: 'That's how the last guy ran it.'

She red bricked half the invite list and trimmed the deck to five key insights. No one missed the old way.

'WHAT IF WE NEED IT LATER?'

This sounds prudent, sensible and risk-aware, but most of the time, it's code for 'I don't want to make the call.'

Could you need it later? Maybe, but the real question is: 'What is it costing you now?' And if it does turn out you need something back, you can always reintroduce it: better, faster and cleaner.

Inaction isn't protection; it's a slow leak.

Priya, an audience member at a conference, came up to me after my talk and shared a story that summed this up perfectly. She was holding onto an old CRM (customer relationship management) system 'just in case' they needed the historical data. It was clunky, expensive and no one on the team had logged in for months. Finally, she archived what mattered, shut it down and saved the business thousands each year. And not once did anyone ask for it back.

Red Brick Thinking at its finest.

'IT MIGHT UPSET SOMEONE.'

It's possible you'll upset someone, but what's the alternative? You keep overloading your team to avoid a few uncomfortable moments? You keep running with cluttered slides, bloated calendars, and tired projects because someone, somewhere, might feel slighted?

A friend of mine, Eli, was in a group chat that had grown from a fun, occasional check-in to a barrage of babble. He didn't want to offend anyone by leaving, so he stayed, muted the thread, but still checked it out of guilt. One night, after reading 47 unread messages about nothing in particular, he quietly exited. No explanation, no drama. The world didn't end. Two people messaged him privately to say they'd been thinking about doing the same.

He red bricked his way to serenity.

Red Brick Thinking is courageous. If you do it with transparency and intent, most people will be relieved rather than offended. People don't want more; they want meaningful.

Most of the resistance to Red Brick Thinking isn't related to the thing you are removing. It's about the discomfort of letting go.

Feel the discomfort then remove that red brick anyway.

SAY IT OUT LOUD

Red Brick Thinking gets even more powerful when you start speaking it into the room.

Language leads culture. When you start using 'red brick' as a verb, people will soon know what you mean, and more importantly, they'll soon start seeing what you see. You move from identifying a red brick you need to remove through to taking action to remove the red brick.

Try it:

- 'Let's red brick this project before we add more.'
- 'Time to red brick our meeting culture.'
- 'We need to red brick our reporting. It's slowing us down.'

It's faster than saying let's streamline, cut back or rethink our approach. It's shorthand for creating space.

When your team starts using red brick as a verb, that's when you know the shift is happening. That's when subtraction becomes part of how you operate.

Don't wait for it to become a buzzword; just say it.

BUILD THE HABIT

This isn't about making one bold decision.

Red Brick Thinking is a practice: something you do again and again until it becomes instinct.

You don't just stumble into clarity — you create it, one brick at a time.

Start with one thing today:

- Cancel a meeting.
- Remove a task.
- Say no.
- Delete the draft you're never going to send.
- Let go of the thing that's not serving you.

Feel the space it creates … then do it again tomorrow.

Before long, you won't be asking, 'Should I add something?' You'll be asking 'What's the red brick here?'

That's when Red Brick Thinking stops being a tool and becomes your default.

Chapter 20

The red brick stops with you

Every practice reaches a tipping point — the moment you stop learning it and start living it.

Red Brick Thinking has taken you through the case for less, the weight of more, the habit of addition and the freedom of subtraction. You've seen the science, the stories, the costs and the traps.

Now, it's up to you.

This isn't about transformation with fanfare. It's about the quiet power of a single choice: the decision to remove a red brick, even when no one asked you to, and even when no one notices.

You don't need to write a business case to remove what no longer belongs. You just need presence and a bit of nerve.

The shift happens not when you understand the idea but when you *act* on it.

RED BRICK THINKING DOESN'T REQUIRE AUTHORISATION

There's a myth we're taught early, especially in workplaces: wait your turn, stay in your lane, change only comes from the top.

Red Brick Thinking cuts through that.

- You don't need a title to stop duplicating documents.

- You don't need approval to cancel a meeting that's lost its purpose.

- You don't need consensus to unsubscribe, simplify, delete or say no.

Every time you make something clearer, cleaner or lighter, you're leading.

Even if no one sees it. Especially if no one sees it.

Vi, a participant from one of my workshops, quietly stopped copying 10 people on every status update email. There was no announcement or policy change; it was just a personal decision to reduce traffic. A month later, the whole team followed. No one missed a thing.

Red Brick Thinking spreads, but it starts with someone choosing to act.

That someone can be you.

NO ONE ELSE IS COMING

Here's the truth most people avoid: no one is going to rescue you from overload, or busyness, or clutter.

- There's no magical meeting where everyone decides to simplify.

- There's no permission slip coming from HR.

- There's no system overhaul designed to make your life feel spacious.

You have to create that space. *You* have to notice the friction. And then, red brick by red brick, *you* have to remove the things that are slowing you down.

This is agency in its truest form. You're not waiting for the system to change, and you're not hoping your boss will finally say, 'That process is a mess.' You're seeing the thing that has drifted from its original intent and letting it go.

If you're carrying too much and struggling under the weight, it's not because you're weak. It's because you've been waiting too long for someone else to lighten the load.

Stop waiting and start removing those red bricks.

THE BRICK MIGHT BE CULTURAL, STRUCTURAL OR EMOTIONAL

Some red bricks are buried deep in your habits, while others are hiding in your self-talk. Many red bricks live in team culture and are disguised as 'how we do things here.'

You might not notice them at first as they're subtle. They sound like:

- 'I have to be across everything.'
- 'If I don't respond instantly, I'm falling behind.'
- 'Saying no makes me look disengaged.'
- 'Busy means important.'

These beliefs are heavy. They don't just fill time; they drain energy and feel personal, but they're often inherited from old bosses, broken systems or years of praise for overwork.

You can red brick those beliefs too:

- Remove the pressure to prove.
- Unsubscribe from perfectionism.
- Stop chasing validation through exhaustion.

Start by noticing the voice in your head that says, 'You can't drop that.' Then, ask yourself: 'Is that true? Or is it just a red brick I've never questioned?'

WHEN YOU RED BRICK, OTHERS NOTICE

When you stop doing things that have outlived their purpose, it doesn't isolate you — it inspires others.

You don't need to convince anyone. You just need to act.

Because when someone sees you say no with confidence, when they see you simplify a process that's been bloated for years, when they hear you question the thing no one else will, they take notice: not because you're loud, but because you're clear.

One department head I spoke with stopped replying to emails after 6pm. She didn't make a fuss about it. She just quietly removed the expectation that responsiveness equals commitment. Within weeks, her team followed suit. No one asked permission — they just felt the shift.

Red Brick Thinking is contagious. The simplest act of subtraction can shift the tone, pace and direction of an entire culture.

So don't underestimate what happens when you start.

WHAT IF EVERYONE DID THIS?

What if every team paused before taking on something new and asked what they could remove first?

What if your workplace normalised 'stop doing' lists alongside to-do lists?

What if saying no was seen as strategic, not selfish?

What if the measure of good was about value, not volume?

- Imagine a project with fewer moving parts and more movement.

- Imagine a calendar with fewer meetings and more thinking.

- Imagine a culture where progress involves prioritising rather than posturing.

This isn't fantasy: this is what happens when people apply Red Brick Thinking consistently, consciously and visibly.

It doesn't take a movement to change a culture. It just takes one person brave enough to remove what no longer belongs.

And guess what? That person is you.

JOIN THE MOVEMENT

Red Brick Thinking is a movement.

It's a way of working, leading and living that begins by asking a powerful question: what no longer needs to be here?

It starts with small, deliberate acts… cancelling a meeting, saying no to a report no one reads or letting go of a role, a rule or a responsibility that has quietly expired.

   Each time we subtract with intention, we create more space for what matters most.

If this thinking has struck a chord with you, I'd love you to join me.

You can work with me through keynotes, workshops, retreats or coaching if you want help building Red Brick Thinking into how you lead, decide and shape your culture. I work with teams and leaders across industries who are ready to clear the noise and move with sharper focus and greater intent.

But this isn't just about what happens in the rooms I'm

This is a conversation, a mindset and a growing movement, and while I'd love to hear how you're red bricking in your world, all you need to do to get started is make some deliberate choices.

So, start saying it out loud.

'I just red bricked ... ':

- An outdated approval step
- A time-wasting meeting
- A bloated document
- A role I've outgrown.

Tag it, share it, post it, pass it on, use the language and start normalising the idea that less is not lazy — it's wise.

This is how the shift spreads.

If you're ready to build your own Red Brick Revolution, you can find me at www.donnamcgeorge.com

Let's make space for what matters. Together.

Book Donna McGeorge to speak at your next event.

REFERENCES

BEFORE WE BEGIN

Smriti (2022). A simple idea that made millions: Swan Vesta matches. InspireIP. https://inspireip.com/capturing-employee-idea-swan-vesta-matchbox/

CHAPTER 1

D McGeorge (2022). *The 1 Day Refund: Take Back Time, Spend It Wisely.* John Wiley & Sons.

GA Adams, BA Converse, A Hales and L Klotz (2022). When subtraction adds value. *Harvard Business Review.*

GS Adams, BA Converse, AH Hales and LE Klotz (2021). People systematically overlook subtractive changes. *Nature,* 592, 258–261.

World Health Organization (2019). Burn-out an 'occupational phenomenon': International Classification of Diseases. https://www.who.int/mental_health/evidence/burn-out/en/

HJ Freudenberger (1974). Staff burn-out. *Journal of Social Issues,* 30(1), 159–165.

World Health Organization, Regional Office for Europe (2022). Putting health at the centre of post-COVID recovery: WHO European Region faces stark choices that will shape its future. https://www.who.int/europe/news/item/10-03-2022-putting-health-at-the-centre-of-post-covid-recovery-who-european-region-faces-stark-choices-that-will-shape-its-future

McKinsey Health Institute (2022). Addressing employee burnout: Are you solving the right problem? https://www.mckinsey.com/mhi/our-insights/addressing-employee-burnout-are-you-solving-the-right-problem

SuperFriend (2023). *Indicators of a Thriving Workplace Survey 2023.* https://www.superfriend.com.au/research/workplace-mental-health-statistics

RE Bohn and JE Short (2009). *How much information? 2009 report on American consumers.* Global Information Industry Center, University of California, San Diego.

Minecheck (2023). Your brain is processing more data than you would ever imagine. https://www.minecheck.com/posts/your-brain-is-processing-more-data-than-you-would-ever-imagine/

E Awh, EK Vogel and S-H Oh (2006). Interactions between attention and working memory. *Neuroscience*, 139(1), 201–208.

Pragmatic Thinking (n.d.). The rise of meeting free workdays. https://pragmaticthinking.com/blog/the-rise-of-meeting-free-workdays/

Humanium (n.d.). Finland's children-centric school system: A global model for success. https://www.humanium.org/en/finlands-children-centric-school-system-a-global-model-for-success/

Herald Sun (2024). This school only teaches students four days a week. Does it work? https://www.heraldsun.com.au/victoria-education/four-day-teaching-week-and-later-starts-for-students-at-st-josephs-college-geelong-proves-great-success/news-story/bbba1fd29bca4398863cbc8557ce2f69

CHAPTER 2

R Tashjian (2021). Why did Bottega Veneta delete its social media accounts? *GQ* magazine. https://www.gq.com/story/bottega-veneta-deletes-social-media

Kering (2022). Excellent 2021 performances, well ahead of 2019 levels. Press release. https://www.kering.com/en/news/excellent-2021-performances-well-ahead-of-2019-levels/

Autonomy (2023). The Results Are In: The UK's Four-Day Week Pilot. https://autonomy.work/portfolio/uk4dwpilotresults/

CHAPTER 3

JD Campbell (1990). Self-esteem and clarity of the self-concept. *Journal of Personality and Social Psychology*, 59(3), 538–549.

D Kahneman, JL Knetsch and RH Thaler (1991). Anomalies: The endowment effect, loss aversion, and status quo bias. *Journal of Economic Perspectives*, 5(1), 193–206.

W Rahula (1974). *What the Buddha Taught* (2nd ed.). Grove Press.

CHAPTER 4

Justologist (2024). How Starbucks failed in Australia: The $105 million loss bet. https://www.justologist.com/how-starbucks-failed-in-australia/

Expert Market Research (2025). Australia Self-Storage Market Size, Share, Growth Analysis Report and Forecast Trends 2025–2034. https://www.expertmarketresearch.com.au/reports/australia-self-storage-market

F Coleman (2023). Decluttering your life can save your mental Health. StudyFinds. https://studyfinds.org/decluttering-mental-health/

M Kituyi and P Thomson (2018). 90% of fish stocks are used up – fisheries subsidies must stop. United Nations Conference on Trade and Development. https://unctad.org/news/90-fish-stocks-are-used-fisheries-subsidies-must-stop

M Igini (2023). 10 concerning fast fashion waste statistics. Earth.org. https://earth.org/statistics-about-fast-fashion-waste/

J Gustavsson, C Cederberg, U Sonesson, R van Otterdijk and A Meybeck (2011). Global Food Losses and Food Waste: Extent, Causes and Prevention. Food and Agriculture Organization of the United Nations. https://www.fao.org/4/mb060e/mb060e.pdf

R Cullen (2024). Why the tiny house movement in Australia is gaining momentum. Instant Living. https://instantliving.com.au/tiny-house-movement-in-australia/

Microsoft (2023). Will AI Fix Work? Work Trend Index Annual Report. https://www.microsoft.com/en-us/worklab/work-trend-index/will-ai-fix-work

D McGeorge (2018). *The 25 Minute Meeting: Half the Time, Double the Impact.* John Wiley & Sons Australia.

J McGregor (2023). This company is canceling all meetings with more than two employees to free up workers' time. *Forbes.*

D McGeorge (2019). *The First 2 Hours: Make Better Use of Your Most Valuable Time.* John Wiley & Sons Australia.

CHAPTER 5

D Gayle (2015). Nick Cave's son took LSD before cliff fall death, inquest hears. *The Guardian.*

M Mordue (2017). Nick Cave: 'I have turned a corner and wandered on to a vast landscape'. *The Guardian.*

M Matousek (2018). Elon Musk says people need to work around 80 hours per week to change the world. *Business Insider.*

C Winfield (2015). This is Warren Buffett's best investment advice. *Time.*

B Creagh (2018). Managing fatigue in mining. Australian Mining.

A Einstein (1945). Letter to Jacques S Hadamard. As cited in Popova, M. (2013). How Einstein thought: 'Combinatory play' and the key to creativity. The Marginalian. https://www.themarginalian.org/2013/08/14/how-einstein-thought-combinatorial-creativity/

R Muller (2018). Bill Gates spends two weeks alone in the forest each year. Here's why. Thrive Global. https://community.thriveglobal.com/bill-gates-think-week/

J Youshaei (2020). Hamilton: How Lin-Manuel Miranda created a hit musical. *Forbes*.

J Desjardins (2023). Visualizing annual working hours in OECD countries. Visual Capitalist. https://www.visualcapitalist.com/annual-working-hours-in-countries-2023/

OECD. (n.d.). Work-life balance – OECD Better Life Index. https://www.oecdbetterlifeindex.org/topics/work-life-balance/

A Fifield (2016). Japanese people 'dying from overwork' by putting in more than 60 hours a week. *The Independent*.

CHAPTER 6

DL Jacobs (2012). Winning the lottery isn't always a happy ending. *Forbes*.

M Gill (2024). Belief in a lottery curse is comforting, but winning lots of money does make you happy. *The Guardian*.

E Crabtree (2023). Lottery winner took home $18 million jackpot but was penniless in a decade and left with just $700 in her account. *The Sun*, US Edition.

RA Easterlin (1974). Does economic growth improve the human lot? Some empirical evidence. In PA David and MW Reder (Eds.), *Nations and Households in Economic Growth: Essays in Honor of Moses Abramovitz* (pp. 89–125). Academic Press.

RA Emmons and ME McCullough (2003). Counting blessings versus burdens: An experimental investigation of gratitude and subjective well-being in daily life. *Journal of Personality and Social Psychology*, 84(2), 377–389.

O Burkeman (2021). *Four Thousand Weeks: Time Management for Mortals*. Farrar, Straus and Giroux.

DH Pink (2009). *Drive: The Surprising Truth About What Motivates Us*. Riverhead Books.

NM Lambert, FD Fincham, TF Stillman and LR Dean (2009). More gratitude, less materialism: The mediating role of life satisfaction. *The Journal of Positive Psychology*, 4(1), 32–42.

S Achor (2010). *The Happiness Advantage: The Seven Principles of Positive Psychology that Fuel Success and Performance at Work*. Broadway Books.

CHAPTER 7

R Catterson (2023). Boxing Day sales bring in $1.3 billion. Power Retail. https://powerretail.com.au/boxing-day-sales-bring-in-1-3-billion/

National Storage (2017). Do Aussies have too much 'stuff'? https://nationalstorage.com.au/blog/aussies-too-much-stuff/

C Palahniuk (1996). *Fight Club*. WW Norton & Company.

RW Belk (1988). Possessions and the extended self. *Journal of Consumer Research*, 15(2), 139–168.

Neuroscience News (2024). Why we buy what we buy: The neuroscience of shopping. Neuroscience News. https://neurosciencenews.com/neuroeconomics-shopping-neuroscience-28247/

M Pigliucci (2017). *How to Be a Stoic: Using Ancient Philosophy to Live a Modern Life*. Basic Books.

S Suzuki (1970). *Zen Mind, Beginner's Mind: Informal Talks on Zen Meditation and Practice*. Weatherhill.

Contemplative Interbeing (2024). The Buddha and St. Francis. https://contemplativeinterbeing.org/2024/06/10/the-buddha-and-st-francis/

JF Millburn and R Nicodemus (2021). *Love People, Use Things: Because the Opposite Never Works*. Celadon Books.

M Kondo (2014). *The Life-Changing Magic of Tidying Up: The Japanese Art of Decluttering and Organizing*. Ten Speed Press.

L Babauta (2009). *The Power of Less: The Fine Art of Limiting Yourself to the Essential… in Business and in Life*. Hyperion.

C Carver (2017). *Soulful Simplicity: How Living with Less can Lead to So Much More*. TarcherPerigee.

F Sasaki (2017). *Goodbye, Things: The New Japanese Minimalism* (E Sugita, Trans.). WW Norton & Company.

A Fernandes (2023). Slow movement: For a world with purpose. Vida Simples. https://vidasimples.co/sustentabilidade/movimento-slow-por-um-mundo-com-proposito/

M Magnusson (2018). *The Gentle Art of Swedish Death Cleaning: How to Free Yourself and Your Family from a Lifetime of Clutter*. Scribner.

Y Murray-Atfield (2019). Australians create 67 million tonnes of waste each year. Here's where it all ends up. ABC News.

CHAPTER 8

J Fried and DH Hansson (2010). *Rework*. Crown Business.

S Sandberg (2013). *Lean In: Women, Work, and the Will to Lead*. Knopf.

J Fried and DH Hansson (2013). *Remote: Office Not Required*. Crown Business.

J Fried and DH Hansson (2018). *It Doesn't Have to Be Crazy at Work*. Harper Business.

PL Hewitt and GL Flett (1991). Perfectionism in the self and social contexts: Conceptualization, assessment, and association with psychopathology. *Journal of Personality and Social Psychology*, 60(3), 456–470.

N Disseldorp (2018). Developing a horrible goose and a huge following. VicScreen. https://vicscreen.vic.gov.au/news/developing-a-horrible-goose-and-a-huge-following

CHAPTER 9

SE Lamond (2024). Canva: How Melanie Perkins built a $40 billion design empire. Medium: The Million Dollar Thinker.

V Turk (2024). Canva revolutionized graphic design. Will it survive the age of AI? Wired. https://www.wired.com/story/canva-ceo-melanie-perkins-interview

RB Zajonc (1968). Attitudinal effects of mere exposure. *Journal of Personality and Social Psychology*, 9(2, Pt.2), 1–27.

E Aronson and J Mills (1959). The effect of severity of initiation on liking for a group. *Journal of Abnormal and Social Psychology*, 59(2), 177–181.

W Samuelson and R Zeckhauser (1988). Status quo bias in decision making. *Journal of Risk and Uncertainty*, 1(1), 7–59.

D Andersen (2012). The Collison brothers and story behind the founding of Stripe. Startup Grind. https://www.startupgrind.com/blog/the-collison-brothers-and-story-behind-the-founding-of-stripe/

CHAPTER 10

TV Central (2023). Bluey on ABC ratings record a season average of 11 million viewers. https://www.tvcentral.com.au/news/abc-news/bluey-on-abc-ratings-record-a-season-average-of-11-million-viewers/

J Whittock (2024). Bluey creator Joe Brumm on making a TV juggernaut, not compromising his vision and the heeler family's future. Deadline. https://deadline.com/2024/04/bluey-joe-brumm-interview-sign-special-episode-1235867154/

DM Oppenheimer (2006). Consequences of erudite vernacular utilized irrespective of necessity: Problems with using long words needlessly. *Applied Cognitive Psychology*, 20(2), 139–156.

A Tversky and D Kahneman (1991). Loss aversion in riskless choice: A reference-dependent model. *The Quarterly Journal of Economics*, 106(4), 1039–1061.

DH Meadows (2008). *Thinking in Systems: A Primer*. Chelsea Green Publishing.

J Beer (2018). Exclusive 'Patagonia is in business to save our home planet.' *Fast Company*.

Y Chouinard (2022). Earth is now our only shareholder. Patagonia. https://www.patagonia.com/ownership

CHAPTER 11

R Hastings (2009). Netflix Culture: Freedom & Responsibility. Netflix slide presentation. https://www.slideshare.net/reed2001/culture-1798664

S Bellezza, N Paharia and A Keinan (2017). Conspicuous consumption of time: When busyness and lack of leisure time become a status symbol. *Journal of Consumer Research*, 44(1), 118–138.

TD Wilson, DA Reinhard, EC Westgate, DT Gilbert, N Ellerbeck, C Hahn, CL Brown and A Shaked (2014). Just think: The challenges of the disengaged mind. *Science*, 345(6192), 75–77.

S David (2016). *Emotional Agility: Get Unstuck, Embrace Change, and Thrive in Work and Life*. Avery.

R Harris (2008). *The Happiness Trap: How to Stop Struggling and Start Living*. Trumpeter.

B Gray, DO Sarnak and J Burgers (2015). Home care by self-governing nursing teams: The Netherlands' Buurtzorg model. The Commonwealth Fund. https://www.commonwealthfund.org/publications/case-study/2015/may/home-care-self-governing-nursing-teams-netherlands-buurtzorg-model

PM DeWitt (2022). *De-implementation: Creating the Space to Focus on What Works*. Corwin Press.

GM Clark (2000). *Sounds from Silence: Graeme Clark and the Bionic Ear Story*. Allen & Unwin.

CHAPTER 12

L Hooker (2024). No films, no music, no sleep: Is 'raw-dogging' long flights heroic or foolish? BBC News. https://www.bbc.com/news/articles/c5y83kj3wg2o

RM Sapolsky (2017). *Behave: The Biology of Humans at Our Best and Worst*. Penguin Press.

A Lembke (2021). *Dopamine Nation: Finding Balance in the Age of Indulgence*. Dutton.

T Harris and A Raskin (2020). 'The Social Dilemma' (Podcast episode). Series: *Your Undivided Attention*. Center for Humane Technology. https://www.humanetech.com/podcast

American Psychological Association (2023). 'Episode 76: The molecule of more — dopamine, with Daniel Lieberman, MD, and Michael Long' (podcast episode). Series: *Speaking of Psychology*. https://www.apa.org/news/podcasts/speaking-of-psychology/dopamine

J Hari (2022). *Stolen Focus: Why You Can't Pay Attention — and How to Think Deeply Again*. Crown Publishing Group.

T Harris (2013). A call to minimize distraction & respect users' attention. Presentation.

H Chandonnet (2023). According to technologists, technology is making it harder for us to focus at work. *Fast Company*.

CHAPTER 13

M Neville (2019). *Shangri-La*. Showtime.

M Zhu, Y Yang and CK Hsee (2018). The mere urgency effect. *Journal of Consumer Research*, 45(3), 673–690.

G Mark, D Gudith and U Klocke (2008). The cost of interrupted work: More speed and stress. *Proceedings of the SIGCHI Conference on Human Factors in Computing Systems* (pp. 107–110). Association for Computing Machinery.

CHAPTER 14

Ferrari. www.ferrari.com

M Mikolajczak and I Roskam (2018). *Le burnout parental: Comprendre, diagnostiquer et prendre en charge*. De Boeck Supérieur.

World Health Organization (2019). Burn-out an 'occupational phenomenon': International Classification of Diseases. https://www.who.int/mental_health/evidence/burn-out/en/

E Nagoski and A Nagoski (2019). *Burnout: The Secret to Unlocking the Stress Cycle*. Ballantine Books.

A Daminger (2019). The cognitive dimension of household labor. *American Sociological Review*, 84(4), 609–633.

B Brown (2010). *The Gifts of Imperfection: Let Go of Who You Think You're Supposed to Be and Embrace Who You Are*. Hazelden Publishing.

R Cross, R Rebele and A Grant (2016). Collaborative overload. *Harvard Business Review*.

C Che (2025). The man making a business out of China's burnout generation. *The Guardian*.

SD Anthony, DS Duncan and PMA Siren (2015). Zombie projects: How to find them and kill them. *Harvard Business Review*.

CHAPTER 15

S Jones (2020). Princess Anne recalls surviving kidnap attempt and telling kidnapper: 'Not bloody likely'. *The Independent*.

C Phillips (2025). *Let Them: Words for the Healing Soul*. Self-published poem.

D Goleman (1995). *Emotional Intelligence: Why It Can Matter More Than IQ*. Bantam Books.

L Stampler (2013). Obama engages hecklers during immigration speech. *Time*.

CHAPTER 16

J Ardern (2023). 'For me, it's time': Jacinda Ardern's resignation speech in full. The Spinoff. https://thespinoff.co.nz/politics/19-01-2023/for-me-its-time-jacinda-arderns-resignation-speech-in-full

K Christie (2023). *The Life List: Master Every Moment and Live an Audacious Life*. Wiley.

N Brantmark (2017). *Lagom (Not Too Little, Not Too Much): The Swedish Art of Living a Balanced, Happy Life*. Harper Design.

CHAPTER 17

ABC News (2022). World No. 1 Ash Barty, 25, announces retirement from tennis: 'I'm so happy and I'm so ready'. ABC News.

AAP (2022). Ash Barty's decision to leave tennis five years ago a blessing in disguise. News.com.au.

E Goffman (1956). *The Presentation of Self in Everyday Life*. Anchor Books.

A Sandemose (1936). *A Fugitive Crosses His Tracks* (E Gay-Tifft, Trans.). AA Knopf.

NT Feather (1989). Attitudes towards the high achiever: The fall of the tall poppy. *Australian Journal of Psychology*, 41(3), 239–267.

CHAPTER 18

J Dokic and J Halloran (2018). *Unbreakable*. Ebury Press.

R Bruner (2021). Here's why Taylor Swift is re-releasing her old albums. *Time*.

Get done in an hour what most people do in a day

With *The ChatGPT Revolution*, you'll learn how easy it is to make AI work for you – with tips and prompts to help you get fast, powerful results in ChatGPT and other AI tools. This is your must-read guide for using generative AI to supercharge your productivity at work, at home and everywhere in between.

AI technologies are here to stay. This book is your invitation to join the revolution.

Printed and bound by CPI Group (UK) Ltd, Croydon, CR0 4YY

22/10/2025

14749194-0001